Workbook

BACKPACK 6

Second Edition

Mario Herrera · Diane Pinkley

PEARSON
Longman

Backpack 6, Second Edition
Workbook

Pearson Education, 10 Bank Street, White Plains, NY 10606, USA

Staff credits: The people who made up the *Backpack 6* Workbook team, representing editorial, production, design, and manufacturing, are Rhea Banker, Carol Brown, Sarah Bupp, Tracey Cataldo, Gina DiLillo, Christine Edmonds, Christopher Leonowicz, Maria Pia Marrella, Linda Moser, Diane Pinkley, Edie Pullman, Nicole Santos, Susan Saslow, and Andrew Vaccaro.

Text composition: TSI Graphics
Text font: 14 pt HSP Helvetica Text
Illustration credits: Adams, Johns, 29, 34; Akib, Jamel, 97; Armstrong, Gail, 51, 61, 63, 64; Barbera, Michelle, 29; Bernatene, Norberto, 43, 90; Boyd, Chris, 54; Clarke, Heather, 17; Diggory, Nick, 42, 51; DK Images, 50; Embleton, Chris, 74; Johnson, Richard, 2, 7, 10, 19, 28, 76, 89; Kemly, Kathleen, 1, 13, KJA.com, 46; Lucas, Katherine, 79; Montiel, Javier, 14, 19, 26, 31, 70, 79, 122; Oliver, Jamie, 41, 62; Richardson, Peter, 6, 40, 49, 82, 91, 99, 101, 106; Ryan, Willie, 5, 28, 44, 86, 89, 90; Smith, Jan, 67; Smith, Richard, 15, 27, 62, 78, 84; Spendor, Nick, 73; Waitzman, William, 31, 65, 66, 106; Willey, Bee, 37, 55, 85, 103; Williams, Sharon, 19, 45, 72, 73, 74, 77, 79, 80, 99; Wright, Luella, 98
Photo credits: 3 © Rex Features/Sipa Press; 4 © Guy Lyon Playfair/Fortean Picture Library, © Hulton Archive/Getty Images; 5 © Everett Collection, © Rex Features/ Lehtikuva, © Ronald Grant Archive; 7 © tk; 16 © www.penniestoprotectpolicedogs.org; 26 © Rex Features/DCA; 33 © P.A. Photos/EPA; 35 © DK Images; 36 © DK Images; 56 © Corbis/Randy Wells; 58 © Airsport Photo Library/David Wootton, © Vallarta-adventures.com; 86 © Rex Features/Tony Kyriacou

ISBN-13: 978-0-13-245152-9
ISBN-10: 0-13-245152-2

PEARSON LONGMAN ON THE WEB

Pearsonlongman.com offers online resources for teachers and students. Access our Companion Websites, our online catalog, and our local offices around the world.

Visit us at **pearsonlongman.com**.

Printed in the United States of America
4 5 6 7 8   V039   13 12 11 10 09

Contents

Amazing People

TRACK 3

A. Listen to the song. Answer the questions with complete sentences.

My Amazing Family

1. What did Uncle Presto do? Why do you think he was amazing?

_____

_____

_____

2. Why was Aunt Kim amazing?

_____

_____

_____

3. What four things did Cousin Pat do for older neighbors?

_____

_____

_____

4. When did Uncle Tony become a hero?

_____

_____

_____

B. How about you?

Who is amazing in your family? Why? _____

_____

_____

2 **Write questions or answers.**

1. Who was John Lennon? What did he do?

_____

_____

2. _____

She was a painter. She painted colorful pictures.

3. Who was Antonio Gaudí? What did he do?

_____

_____

4. _____

He was a kung-fu expert. He acted in martial arts films.

3 **Read. Answer the questions.**

Some people are amazing because they do unusual things. Take Englishman Alexander Wortley, for example. He lived in a box until his death in 1980 at the age of 80. His "home sweet home" was a green box only one meter wide, a meter and a half deep, and a little more than a meter and a half tall. Inside, he could not lie down or stand up completely. He made his home out of a wooden box. He used a curved piece of metal for a roof. Because he added four wheels, he could move whenever he wanted to. And Wortley never had to pay rent!

Who was Alexander Wortley? What did he do?

_____

_____

_____

Who **was** Frida Kahlo?   She **was** a painter.
Where **did** she **live**?   She **lived** in Mexico City.
When **did** they **make** a movie about her life?   They **made** it in 2002.

---

4 **Write a verb from the box in the simple past.
Use some verbs more than once.**

act
be
design
live
score
star
win

1. Alexander Wortley _____ an amazing person. He _____ in a box!

2. Antonio Gaudí _____ an architect. He _____ parks and buildings.

3. Salma Hayek and Michael J. Fox are actors. He _____ in the
   Back to the Future movies, and Hayek _____ in the movie *Frida*.

4. The Beatles _____ musicians. They _____ seven Grammy awards.

5. Bruce Lee _____ a kung-fu expert. He _____ in martial arts films.

6. Pelé _____ a soccer player. He _____ 1,281 goals.

5 **Write a question for each statement in Exercise 4.**

1. Who _was Alexander Wortley?_

2. Where _did he live?_

3. Who _____

4. What _____

5. Who _____

6. What _____

7. Who _____

8. How many _____

9. Who _____

10. What _____

11. Who _____

12. How many _____

6 **Complete the timeline with events from the article.**

An Amazing Composer

Franz Liszt, the famous composer, died in 1886. But thirty-seven years later, in 1923, something amazing happened. An Englishwoman, Rosemary Brown, says she saw his spirit! Brown was just seven years old then and didn't know who the spirit was. Ten years later, she saw a picture of Liszt in a book. He was the spirit she had seen! Many years later, in 1964, Brown says Liszt returned and gave her compositions he wrote after his death. Some time later, he introduced her to the spirits of Bach, Beethoven, Chopin, Mozart, and other composers. They also asked her to write down the music they composed after their deaths. Brown had only studied music for two years, but she wrote down more than 500 pieces of music. Many experts believed the dead composers, in fact, had written the compositions. Finally, Brown recorded the album of spirit compositions in 1971. Rosemary Brown died in November 2001.

Franz Liszt

Rosemary Brown

1886 _____

1923 _____

1933 _____

1964 _____

1971 _____

2001 _____

7 **Do the crossword puzzle. Use the words that complete the sentences.**

Across

1. Pelé ___ 1,281 goals.
2. Alexander Wortley ___ in a box.
3. Michael J. Fox ___ in *Back to the Future* movies.
4. The Beatles ___ seven Grammy awards.
5. Jackie Chan ___ at the Peking Opera School.
6. Sarah Chang ___ with an orchestra when she was eight.

Down

7. Antonio Gaudí ___ parks and buildings.
8. Salma Hayek ___ in the movie *Frida*.
9. J.K. Rowling ___ her first book when she was six years old.
10. Rosemary Brown ___ an album of music by dead composers.
11. Kahlo ___ colorful pictures.
12. Dr. Mae Jemison ___ in outer space.

8 **Write. Which person in this unit is the most amazing to you? Why?**

_____

_____

_____

_____

_____

Amazing Person of the Week

Read the magazine *Weird World*.

9 **Check *True* or *False*.**

Strange But True! / Our Readers Write Us

	True	False
1. Michel Lotito was born in France.	☐	☐
2. Lotito only eats metal.	☐	☐
3. Wolfgang Mozart constructed the first piano.	☐	☐
4. Apicius walked 870 miles on his hands.	☐	☐
5. Isilay Davaz began flying lessons at age two.	☐	☐
6. Bill Harding made clothes out of real grass.	☐	☐
7. Marcus Hooper spent $12 million for one party.	☐	☐

10 **Research and write.**

Find out about amazing people who set world records. Look for information on the Internet or at the library. Use the *Guinness World Records* book. Find out about the biggest, smallest, longest, shortest, fastest, slowest of just about anything. Write a paragraph about one person who set a record. Write a title and a topic sentence below. Then write your paragraph on a separate piece of paper. Be sure to answer these questions in your paragraph and draw an illustration.

1. Who set the record?
2. What record did the person set?
3. Why is the record amazing?

_____
(title)

_____

_____

_____

_____

11 Listen. Answer the questions.

1. What did Bethany want to be when she grew up?

   _____

2. How old was Bethany when the accident happened?

   _____

3. What happened to her on October 31st, 2003?

   _____

4. What did she do to save her own life?

   _____

5. When did Bethany get back into the water and begin surfing again?

   _____

6. Do you think she is a hero? Why or why not?

   _____

12 A. Listen. Write the missing simple past verbs.

Dreams

I dreamed I was an astronaut and _____ in outer space.

I _____ all the planets to find my favorite place.

I dreamed I was a painter who _____ scenery.

I _____ my paintings in museums for everyone to see.

I dreamed I was a movie star who _____ a fancy car.

I always _____ dark glasses and _____ near and far.

I dreamed I _____ in business and a well-known VIP.

I _____ my name and I _____—my teacher _____ on me.

B. Write another verse.

I dreamed I was a _____ who _____. I _____ and I _____.

Writing

Biographical Paragraph

A paragraph you write about the life of someone else is called a *biography*. When you write about someone else, you can include facts and important events in the person's life. You present the events and dates in chronological order and use the third person (*he* or *she*). When you write this kind of paragraph, you should include a title and the parts of a paragraph: the topic sentence, detail sentences, and a concluding sentence.

J.K. Rowling: Wizard Writer

Joanne K. Rowling is one of the best children's writers today. She was born on July 31, **1965**, in Chipping Sodbury, near Bristol, England. As a child, she knew she wanted to be a writer. When she was about **six years old**, she wrote her first story, titled *Rabbit*. As the years passed, she finished two novels, but she never tried to get them published. In **1991**, when she was **twenty-six**, she went to Portugal to teach English. At that time, Rowling started writing her third novel, a story about a boy named Harry who had some very special powers. She stopped working on the book when she got married. Later, after the birth of her daughter in **1993**, she moved to Edinburgh, Scotland, and decided to finish her novel. In June **1997**, her first book in the Harry Potter series, *Harry Potter and the Sorcerer's Stone*, was published in England. In **1998** the book appeared in the United States and received excellent reviews. That year the book won many awards, among them The British Book Award for the *Children's Book of the Year*, and the *Smarties Prize*. Between **1998 and 2007**, six more books were added to the Harry Potter series. Rowling's books, now in 64 languages, are sold in America, Brazil, the Czech Republic, England, France, Germany, Italy, Holland, Greece, Finland, Portugal, Denmark, Spain, and Sweden, among other countries. J.K. Rowling is clearly one of the world's most popular writers.

Writing Assignment

Using the following steps, you will write a biographical paragraph about a friend, classmate, or person in your family. You should remember to include important events and dates that make the person's life interesting.

 Brainstorm Ideas

- Who do you want to write about?
- What events were important and/or interesting in the person's life?
- When did the events take place?

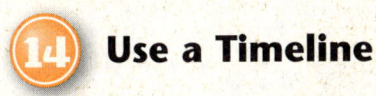 **Use a Timeline**

Interview the person you want to write about. Ask *Wh-* questions.
Write the dates and facts on a timeline, using complete sentences
to help you organize the information.

J.K. Rowling

- 1965   Joanne K. Rowling was born on July 31ˢᵗ.

- 1971   She wrote her first story, called <u>Rabbit</u>.

- 1991   She went to Portugal to teach English.

- 1993   Her daughter was born.

- 1997   <u>Harry Potter and the Sorcerer's Stone</u> was published in England.

- 1998   <u>Harry Potter and the Sorcerer's Stone</u> appeared in the United States. The book won The British Book Award for the <u>Children's Book of the Year</u> and the <u>Smarties Prize</u>.

- 1998–2007   Six more Harry Potter books were published.

_____

- _____   _____
- _____   _____
- _____   _____
- _____   _____
- _____   _____
- _____   _____

To help you . . .

Wh- Questions:	*What* (happened)?	*Where* (did it happen)?
	When (did it happen)?	*Why* (did it happen)?

State and Action Verbs:
be   become   begin   build   have   live   make   move   study

Writing Tip:
Name the person you're writing about in your topic sentence.

 **Write**

Use your timeline to help you write your biographical paragraph. Use a
separate piece of paper.

Review

16 **A. Interview a friend or a person in your family who did something amazing or can tell you about an amazing person. Write down some questions you'd like to ask about the amazing person.**

What _____

When _____

Where _____

How _____

Why _____

B. Ask the person your questions. Take notes. Then complete this timeline about the amazing person.

Amazing Person Timeline

year	what the person did
_____	_____
	_____
	_____
_____	_____
	_____
	_____
_____	_____
	_____
	_____
_____	_____
	_____
	_____
_____	_____
	_____

Communication Activity

Work with a partner: Student A uses this information and Student B turns to page 12.

Student A
Ask questions about amazing "firsts" and the amazing people behind them.
Write the answers.
Answer your partner's questions.

What?	Who?	When?
first croissants	Bakers in Vienna	1863
first newspapers	Roman emperor Julius Caesar	59 B.C.E.
first bus		
first submarine	Dutch inventor Cornelius Drebbel	1620
first watch		
first tea	Chinese emperor Shen Nung	before 2737 B.C.E.
first radio		
first movies	Englishman Eadweard Muybridge in California	1880
first TVs		
first chants	Bishop Ambrose in Milan, Italy	4th century
first aspirin		

Students work with partners to ask and answer questions. Student A uses the information on page 11 and Student B uses the information on page 12. Students use the conversation shown as a model. Students write down their partner's answers. This procedure should be used for other similar Communication Activities at the end of the units in this workbook.

Communication Activity

Work with a partner: Student B uses this information and Student A turns to page 11.

Student B
Answer your partner's questions.
Ask questions about amazing "firsts" and the amazing people behind them.
Write the answers.

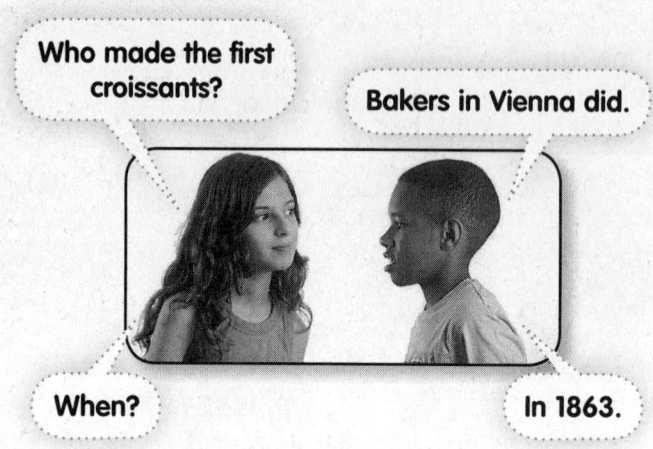

What?	Who?	When?
first croissants	Bakers in Vienna	1863
first newspapers		
first bus	Sir Goldsworthy Gurney in England	1830
first submarine		
first watch	Peter Henlein in Germany	1500
first tea		
first radio	thirty-three-year-old American Lee Deforest	1906
first movies		
first TVs	John Logie Baird in England	1925
first chants		
first aspirin	German Hermann Dresser	1893

Our Stories

TRACK 6

1

A. Listen to the song. Check the things that are true about Kwan.

All About Me

_____ 1. He was born in Busan.

_____ 2. He's lived in Busan since he was small.

_____ 3. He's had a boring childhood.

_____ 4. Kwan has known Shin since 2004.

_____ 5. Kwan and Shin are like family.

_____ 6. Shin and Kwan have played music together.

_____ 7. Kwan plays the keyboard.

_____ 8. Shin plays the keyboard.

B. Write about yourself.

1. I've gone to this school for _____.

2. I've played _____

   for _____.

3. I've lived in _____

   since _____.

4. I've studied _____

   since I was _____.

5. I've known my best friend _____

   since _____.

Glue or draw a picture of yourself here.

Read. Write complete sentences.

1. Min is 12 years old now. She and her family live in Chicago.
   They moved from Korea to Chicago when she was
   two years old.

   Have Min and her family lived in Chicago for a long time?
   Tell why.

   _____

   _____

   Did Min live in Korea for a long time? Tell why.

   _____

   _____

2. Antonio has only had his violin for six months. He's practiced
   the violin every day! Before he got the violin, he played the
   piano. But he only practiced the piano on weekends.

   Has Antonio had his violin for a long time? Tell why.

   _____

   _____

   Which do you think Antonio has enjoyed playing
   more—the violin or the piano? Tell why.

   _____

   _____

3. Maria has known Carla for six years. They are in the same class,
   but they weren't friendly until last year. That's when they started
   to study together. Maria didn't have a pet, but Carla did. Carla
   had a parrot. A few months after they became friends, Maria got
   a parrot, too.

   Have Maria and Carla been friends for a long time? Tell why.

   _____

   _____

   Has Maria had a parrot for a long time? Tell why.

   _____

   _____

How long **has** Carla **known** Maria?
She**'s known** Maria since kindergarten.
She**'s known** Maria for six years.

She's = She has

3 **Write. Use the correct form of a verb from the box.**

be
have
know
live
play

1. David _'s been_____ in this class since last year.

2. Sarah _____ a kitten since July.

3. How long _____ Tamila _____ the guitar?

4. How long _____ Steven _____ Miguel?

5. They _____ in Mexico City for six years.

4 **Read. Write complete questions or answers.**

Sonia is 11 years old. She lives in Mexico City. She moved there when she was eight. Sonia met José two years ago. He is also 11. José was born in Mexico City. José and Sonia like to act in plays. They both started acting last year. They started after their friend Emilio took them to his acting class. Emilio started acting five years ago when he was just six years old.

1. How many years has Sonia lived in Mexico City?

   _She's lived there for three years._____

2. How long has José lived in Mexico City?

   _____

3. _____

   Sonia has known José for two years.

4. _____

   They have been acting since last year.

5. How long has Emilio been acting?

   _____

Amount of time	Specific time
three years	2001
ten minutes	fourth grade
two months	October

first grade	four hours
May	nine o'clock
October 15th	six years
three weeks	two months

 Write the times from the box in the correct column of the chart.

Specific Time	Amount of Time
first grade	

Grammar

When did Henry meet Sally? Henry met Sally **in second grade.**	**How long** has Henry known Sally? He has known her **for four years.** He has known her **since second grade.**

 Use information from the chart to write answers. Write complete sentences.

Name	What?	When? or How Long?
Susan	live in this city	three years
Dan	start to play the piano	second grade
Ron	get his bike	he was seven
Rebecca	go to this school	2002

1. How long has Susan lived in this city?

_____

2. When did Dan start to play the piano?

_____

3. How long has Ron had his bike?

_____

4. How long has Rebecca gone to this school?

_____

7 **A. Complete the sentences with the correct form of the verb.**

Carlos is 11 years old. He was born in Monterrey, Mexico, and has
1 (live) _____ there all of his life. He has **2** (study) _____
English for six years at the English Club. He has **3** (meet) _____ many
friends at the club. They have **4** (play) _____ baseball, soccer, and
tennis together. They have been on the same team, and they have **5** (win)
_____ all the games they've played! Roberto is Carlos's very best friend.
He has **6** (know) _____ him since he was little.

B. Find and circle the words you wrote.

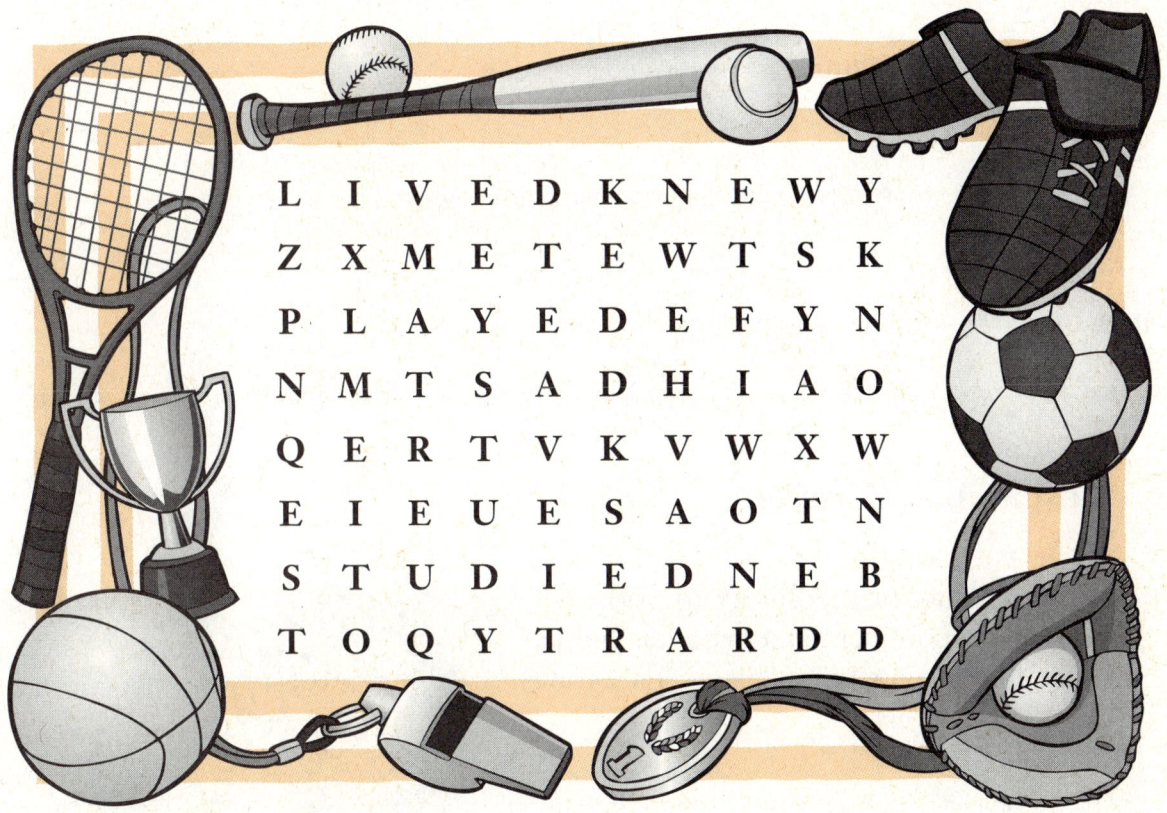

L	I	V	E	D	K	N	E	W	Y
Z	X	M	E	T	E	W	T	S	K
P	L	A	Y	E	D	E	F	Y	N
N	M	T	S	A	D	H	I	A	O
Q	E	R	T	V	K	V	W	X	W
E	I	E	U	E	S	A	O	T	N
S	T	U	D	I	E	D	N	E	B
T	O	Q	Y	T	R	A	R	D	D

C. Use some of the circled words to write about yourself, your family, or your friends.

_____

_____

_____

_____

Read the magazine *Kid Life*.

 Answer the questions.

Guest Editor of the Month

1. What experience has Samantha Green written about? _____

2. How long has she lived in Toronto? _____

3. What question did she ask readers first? _____

4. When did she learn to scuba dive? _____

Kids with Cool Ideas

5. What has Stacey Hillman always loved?

_____

6. When did she start Pennies to Protect Police Dogs?

_____

7. How much money has she collected so far?

_____

(9) **Research and write.**

A. Use the Internet or the library to find information about someone who has helped the world become a better place. Take notes.

   1. When was the person born?

   2. How has the person helped to make the world a better place?

   3. How long has the person helped?

   4. Has the person won a prize or an award?

B. Write a paragraph about the person you researched. Use a separate piece of paper. Present your work to a partner.

 **Listen. Complete the sentences.**

1. Alfredo _____ in Quito, Ecuador, since _____.
2. His family _____ their house for _____.
3. He _____ his best friend Pedro since _____.
4. He _____ soccer, his favorite sport, for _____.
5. He _____ piano lessons since _____.

Quito ★

ECUADOR

 **A. Choose and write rhyming words from the box. Then listen to the chant and check.**

My So-called Story

I was born in this same town.

I've lived right here since _____.

I have a typical mother and father

    and a sister who just turned _____.

I have a dog that I named Spot.

I've had him since I was _____.

He always follows me to school,

    and sometimes makes me _____.

I like to swim and play baseball,

    and I've played soccer for six _____.

I guess my life is just average.

I'm sorry to bore you to _____!

eight	hears
late	tears
ten	then
wait	when
years	

B. Write about you.

I was born in _____.

I've lived right here since _____.

I have a _____ and _____

and a _____ who just turned _____.

Writing

Autobiographical Paragraph

A paragraph you write about yourself is called an *autobiography*. When you write about yourself, you can tell when and where you were born, where you live, and where you go to school. To make your writing more interesting, you can also include details about your likes and dislikes and favorite activities.

All About Me
by Mi-jin Lee

I was born in Japan on June 5th, 1998. I am the youngest of five children. I have three older brothers and an older sister. My family has lived in the United States for almost two years now. Before that, we lived in Tokyo. That city is as busy as New York City. When I was in Japan, I played on a soccer team. Every year our team made it to the finals. I have played soccer since I was five years old. I don't play soccer anymore. Now I play on a tennis team. I also play the piano. I have taken piano lessons for almost a year. I don't like to practice the piano, but my parents feel it is important for me to learn. I've been in English Club since we moved to the United States. A lot of kids my age are in the club. Many of them came from Japan. I've learned a lot of new words since I've been in the club. My brothers have helped me a lot. I've also made a lot of new friends. I love living in the United States, but I miss my old friends in Japan.

Writing Assignment

Using the following steps, you will write a paragraph about yourself. You should include personal details to help the reader get to know you as you write about your feelings and experiences.

 Brainstorm Ideas

- Tell where and when you were born.
- Tell where you live and where you go to school.
- Tell about what you like and don't like to do.
- Tell about your favorite activities.

 Use an Outline

An outline can help you organize your ideas. It helps you state the main ideas (*A, B, C*) and the descriptive details that support the main ideas (*1, 2, 3*). You can state information or facts in complete sentences, or list them in the form of single items or notes. Read Mi-jin's outline on the next page. Then fill out an outline about yourself.

Outline: Mi-jin Lee	
A. Personal History	**B.** My Activities
1. I was born on June 5th, 1998.	1. soccer team
2. I was born in Tokyo, Japan.	2. piano
3. There are five children in my family.	3. tennis
4. I have three older brothers and an older sister.	4. English Club
5. I moved to the United States two years ago.	**C.** Likes and Dislikes
	1. like to play soccer
	2. like to play tennis
	3. don't like to practice the piano

Outline: _____

A. Personal History

  1. I was born on _____

  2. I was born in _____

  3. There are _____ in my family

  4. I have _____ sister(s) and _____ brother(s)

  5. I live _____

B. My Activities

  1. _____

  2. _____

  3. _____

C. Likes and Dislikes

  1. like to _____

  2. don't like to _____

┌─ To help you . . . ─────────────────────────────

State and Action Verbs:

attend   be   do   go   know   learn   live   play   practice   study   win

Time Expressions:

for   six days, two years, a week, a long time

since   the year 2008, last year, September, I can remember

└──

(14) Write

Use your outline to help you write your autobiographical paragraph. Use a separate piece of paper.

A. Read. Write complete questions or answers.

Ben has been on the library steps since two o'clock. It is now three o'clock. Where is Kevin? Ben has known Kevin since they were two years old. Ben knows that Kevin has *always* been late. That's *not* a good habit for a twelve-year-old boy.

Ben and Kevin have studied together for the past four years. They have played on the same soccer team. They have been in the same math class for two years. They have always been best friends!

Maybe this time Kevin just forgot to meet Ben at the library to study for their *last* math test.

1. How long has Ben been on the library steps?

_____

2. _____

Ben and Kevin have known each other since they were two years old.

3. _____

They've studied together for the past four years.

4. How long have Ben and Kevin been best friends?

_____

5. _____

Ben and Kevin have been in the same math class for two years.

B. Write about your best friend. Use *for* or *since*.

_____

_____

_____

_____

Communication Activity

Work with a partner: Student A uses this information and Student B uses the information on page 24.

Student A
Ask questions using *how long?* or *when?* Write the answers.
Answer your partner's questions.

How long has Sacha known Carlos?

She's known Carlos for six years.

When did she meet him?

She met him in 2003.

Who?	What?	How long . . . ? When?
Sacha and Carlos	know each other	*six years / 2003*
Maria and José	play soccer	four years
Kate and Susan	be friends	
Mario and Martin	be neighbors	ten years
Steve and Sarah	go to the same school	
Paula and Pat	start dancing lessons	2001
Joan and Kim	win first place in skating	
Lin	get a pet	2002
Yoko	get new glasses	
Diane	move here	2003
Pedro	get a new bike	

Communication Activity

Work with a partner: Student B uses this information and Student A uses the information on page 23.

Student B
Answer your partner's questions.
Ask questions using *how long?* or *when?* Write the answers.

How long has Sacha known Carlos?

She's known Carlos for six years.

When did she meet him?

She met him in 2003.

Who?	What?	How long . . . ? When?
Sacha and Carlos	know each other	six years / 2003
Maria and José	play soccer	
Kate and Susan	be friends	they were both five years old
Mario and Martin	be neighbors	
Steve and Sarah	go to the same school	they were both six years old
Paula and Pat	start dancing lessons	
Joan and Kim	win first place in skating	1999
Lin	get a pet	
Yoko	get new glasses	last month
Diane	move here	
Pedro	get a new bike	two years ago

Skills and Abilities

 **A. Listen to the song. Answer the questions with complete sentences. Use words from the box.**

A Working Family

biologist
lawyer
musician
reporter
salesperson
vet

1. What does his uncle do?

   His uncle's a salesperson.

2. What does his aunt do?

   _____

3. What does his father do?

   _____

4. What does his mother do?

   _____

5. What does his sister do?

   _____

6. What does his brother do?

   _____

**B. What do the people in your family do?
Fill in the word map.**

My Family's Occupations

2 **A. Complete the sentences. Use phrases from the box.**

designing buildings
helping sick animals
playing basketball
playing music
presenting news
reading books
studying science
working with customers
working with kids
writing about sports

1. I enjoy _____.

   Maybe I'll become a vet.

2. I love _____.

   Maybe I'll become a musician.

3. I love _____.

   Maybe I'll become a professional athlete.

4. I like _____.

   Maybe I'll become a teacher.

5. _____ is my favorite hobby

   Maybe I'll become a librarian.

6. I enjoy _____.

   Maybe I'll become a sports writer.

7. _____ is really cool.

   Maybe I'll become an architect.

8. _____ is great.

   Maybe I'll become a biologist.

9. I like _____.

   Maybe I'll become a salesperson.

10. _____ is interesting.

   Maybe I'll become a reporter.

B. Write about you.

I like _____.

Maybe I'll become _____.

26

Gerund as subject
Reading is my favorite hobby.
Playing the guitar is lots of fun.

Gerund as object
I really enjoy **reading**.
I love **playing** the guitar.

gerund: verb + -*ing*

3 **Complete the sentences. Then circle S for *subject* or O for *object*.**

1. _____ old cars is my uncle's hobby. (fix)   S   O

2. I really like _____ cartoons. (draw)   S   O

3. Bob enjoys _____ volleyball a lot. (play)   S   O

4. _____ stamps is a great hobby. (collect)   S   O

5. Pat doesn't like _____ TV at all. (watch)   S   O

Grammar

excited about ⎤
good at ⎥
interested in ⎥ + gerund
worried about ⎦

I am **excited about playing** the flute.
I am **good at making** clothes.
I am **interested in building** models.
I am **worried about passing** the test.

4 **Unscramble the sentences. Use the gerund.**

1. about / their / they / worried / project / are / finish / on time

_____

2. fix / my / computers / uncle / good / is / at

_____

3. cousin / learn / tae-kwon-do / my / is / in / interested

_____

4. am / about / in / concert / I / sing / excited / the

_____

5 Write sentences. Use words and phrases from the box.

Who's good at what?	
architect	design buildings
carpenter	fix cars
coach	play piano
mechanic	teach sports
pianist	type letters
secretary	work with wood

1. ___An architect is good at designing buildings.___

2. _____

3. _____

4. _____

5. _____

6. _____

Grammar

if + present	*will* + verb
If you **study** hard,	you**'ll pass** the test.
If she **has** time,	she**'ll help** me with my project.
If they **work** hard,	they**'ll get** good grades.

6 Complete the sentences. Use the simple present and the future with a contraction (*'ll*).

1. If you _____ that art class,   you _____ art supplies.
   (take)   (need)

2. If he _____ the time,   he _____ me his model ships.
   (have)   (show)

3. If they _____ hard,   they _____ the soccer game.
   (practice)   (win)

4. If I _____ enough money,   I _____ a new guitar.
   (save)   (buy)

5. If she _____ on the Internet,   she _____ that information.
   (look)   (find)

28

Complete the sentences.

1. If Martin saves enough money, he _____.

2. If you study this book, you _____.

3. If they have the time, they _____.

4. If _____, your teacher will be happy.

5. If _____, we'll win first prize.

6. If _____, I'll speak English well.

 Complete the puzzle with words from the box.

Across

1. If you're ____, you'll see things other people don't.
2. If you're ____, you can wait for a long time without getting upset.
3. If you have ____ ability, you'll do well in physics class.
4. If you're ____, you'll make your friends laugh.

Down

5. If you're ____, you won't have any accidents.
6. If you're ____, you'll get good grades.
7. If you're ____, you'll do well in drawing class.
8. If you're ____, you'll feel nervous and embarrassed sometimes.

artistic
careful
funny
mathematical
observant
patient
sensitive
smart

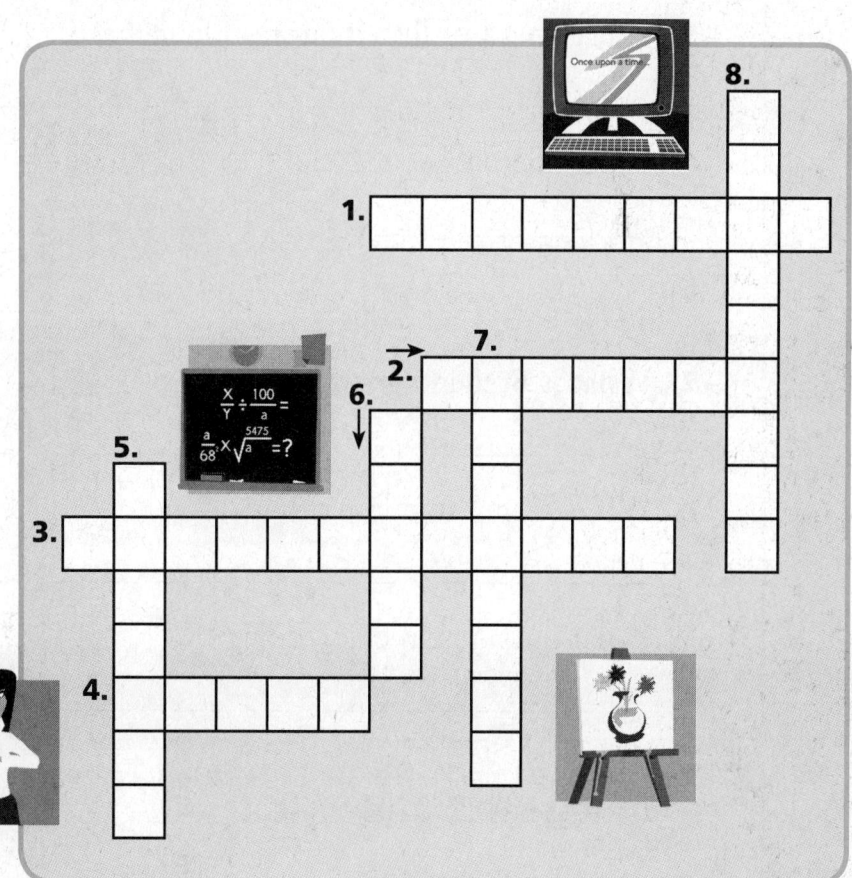

Read *Cool Kids Magazine*.

 Answer each question with a complete sentence.

Kids Making News!

1. Where can children work as reporters?

_____

2. Where and when did this organization start?

_____

3. Where do the kids' articles appear?

_____

How Cool Is This?

4. What does a games tester do?

_____

5. What does Lea like about testing games?

_____

6. What doesn't Lea like about testing games?

_____

Cool Kids with Cool Skills

7. What is Brandon good at doing?

_____

8. Who is interested in writing?

_____

9. What does Austin enjoy doing?

_____

 Research and write.

Use the library or the Internet to find information about another cool kid.
Write a paragraph about that person's special skills.

TRACK 10

11 **Listen and circle the letter *a*, *b*, or *c*.**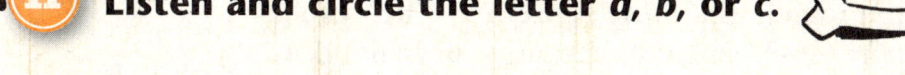

1. Larry is interested in

    a. playing chess.   b. digging for dinosaur bones.   c. learning karate.

2. Sarah's brother is good at

    a. fixing the computer.   b. making cookies.   c. explaining math.

3. Martha is bad at

    a. planning parties.   b. following directions.   c. driving a car.

4. Dolores is worried about

    a. hiding the broken plate.   b. getting sick.   c. passing her test.

TRACK 11

12   **Match. Then listen to the chant and check your answers.**

Everyone Works

  <u> c </u> **1.** Mechanics   a. like helping children with measles.

  _____**2.** Teachers   b. like jumping and running around tracks.

  _____**3.** Actors   c. like working with tools.

  _____**4.** Writers   d. like dancing around on a stage.

  _____**5.** Accountants   e. like drawing and painting on easels.

  _____**6.** Athletes   f. like writing for news magazines.

  _____**7.** Artists   g. like working with numbers and facts.

  _____**8.** Doctors   h. like working in schools.

  _____**9.** Dancers   i. like acting on stages and screens.

13   **Write two more lines for the chant.**

Basketball players like _____.

And I enjoy _____ best of all.

Writing

Paragraph Unity

When you write a paragraph, check to be sure that all of the sentences in it tell about the main idea. The information you include should focus on one topic. You express your **main idea** in the **topic sentence**. Then you use **related details** in the supporting sentences to expand your main idea.

My Future Profession
by Sylvia Gutierrez

Ever since I was a little girl, I have always wanted to work for a newspaper. My grandfather was a reporter for our town's small newspaper, and I used to love visiting the building where everything happened—the reporting, the editing, and the printing of the finished product. He encouraged me to develop the skills and abilities I would need to be a reporter some day. Like him, I enjoy meeting people and talking to them, and I am interested in listening to the stories they tell. I'm also good at asking the right kinds of questions to get the information I need. And I'm not worried about having a deadline to turn in my work. In fact, I like working under pressure. That is why I am a reporter for our school newspaper now. I want to get as much experience as I can, and learn all I can about newspaper reporting. If I continue to write articles for school newspapers all the way through college, I'll have enough experience to get a job as a reporter for our town's newspaper. I'll have my dream job at last!

Writing Assignment

Using the following steps, you will write a paragraph about a job you would like to have one day. Be sure to describe the skills, abilities, and other qualifications you need to do the job. Remember to tell how you became interested in this job and why you want to do it in the future.

 ### Brainstorm Ideas

- Which jobs do you think are interesting and exciting?
- What skills or abilities are necessary to do these jobs?
- What other qualities do you need for these jobs?

 ### Use an Idea Map

Choose a job. Think about the skills, abilities, and qualities that you need for the job. An idea map is a good way to organize your ideas. Look at Sylvia's idea map for newspaper reporting on the next page and then do one of your own.

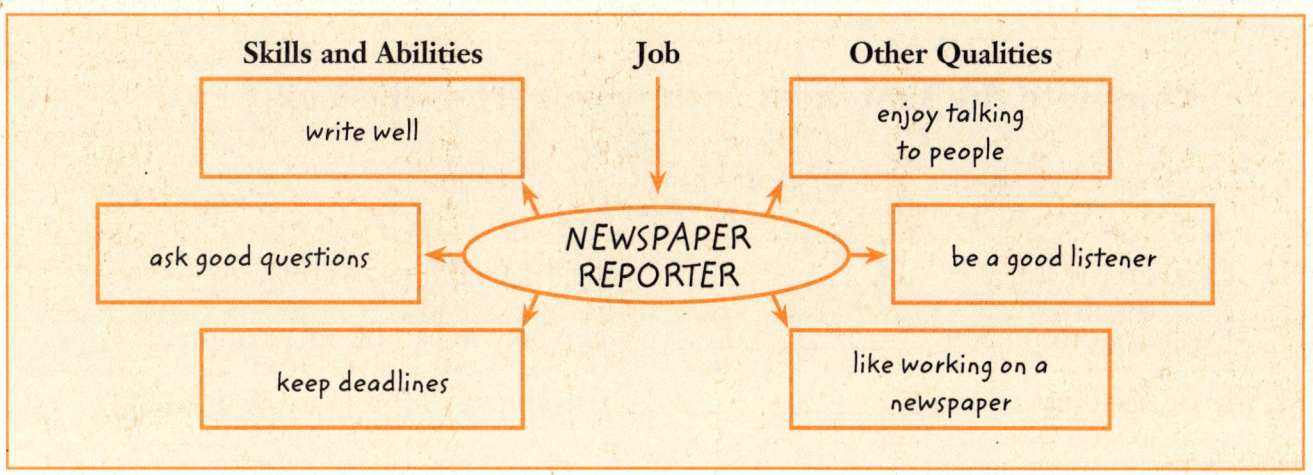

Skills and Abilities

write well

ask good questions

keep deadlines

Job

NEWSPAPER REPORTER

Other Qualities

enjoy talking to people

be a good listener

like working on a newspaper

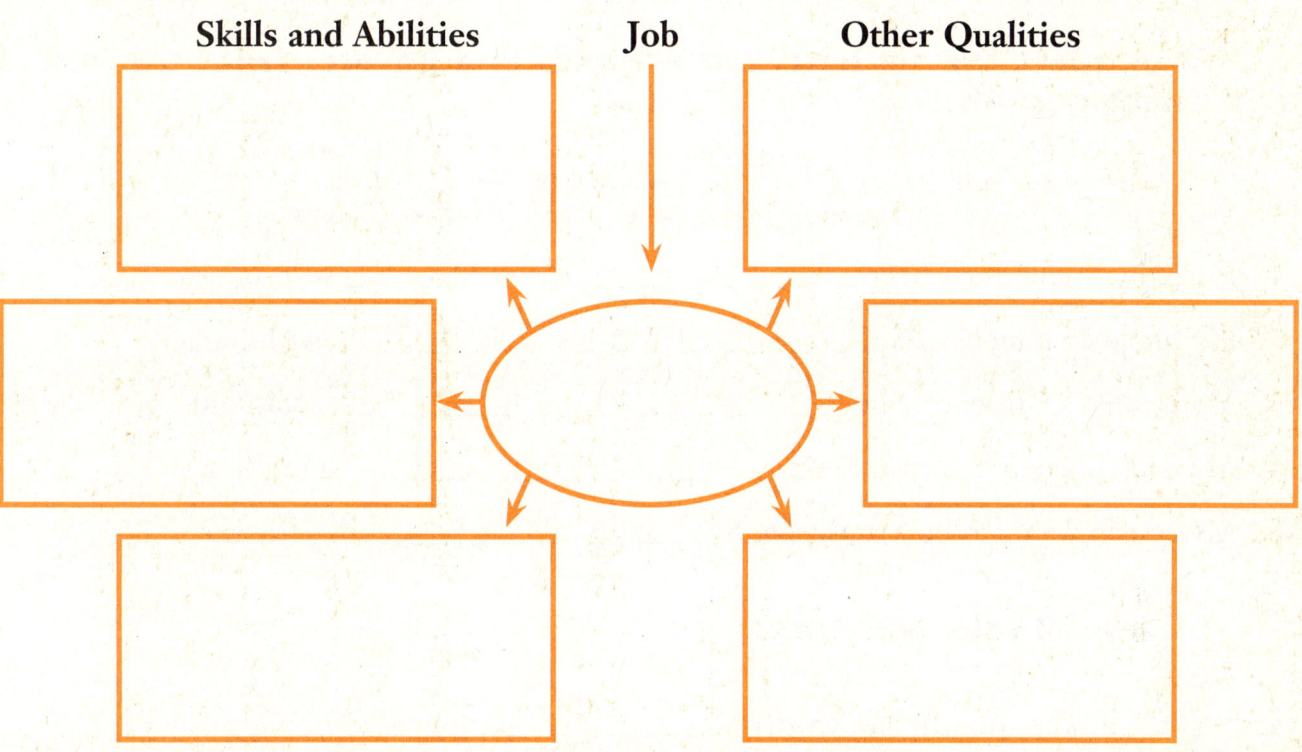

Skills and Abilities

Job

Other Qualities

To help you . . .

Occupation Words:

accountant	actor	athlete	biologist	carpenter	coach
doctor	lawyer	mechanic	musician	photographer	salesperson
set designer	teacher	translator	vet	wait person	writer

Action Words:

| act | design | find | fix | help | make |
| play | read | take | teach | work | write |

 **Write**

Use your idea map to help you write your paragraph.
Use a separate piece of paper.

Review

17 **Complete the sentences with words from the box.**

| artistic | energetic | mathematical | observant |

1. If you are strong and _____, maybe you'll be an athlete one day.

2. If you are careful and _____, maybe you can be an accountant.

3. If you are creative and _____, maybe you'll be an artist one day.

4. If you are outgoing and _____, maybe you can be a reporter.

18 **Complete the sentences. Use words and phrases from the box with gerunds.**

| be excited about | be good at | be interested in | enjoy | love |

1. My aunt's a librarian. She _____ with books.

2. My uncle's a plumber. He _____ with tools.

3. My mother's a teacher. She _____ with kids.

4. My dad's a paleontologist. He _____ with bones.

5. My cousin wants to be a musician. She _____ the flute.

19 **Complete the sentences.**

1. If you help me with my homework, I _____.

2. If I can get a guitar, I _____.

3. If _____, we'll pass the course.

20 **Write about a job you want to have one day. Use _enjoy_ and _good at_.**

_____

_____

_____

_____

_____

Communication Activity

Work with a partner: Student A uses this information and Student B uses the information on page 36.

Student A
Ask questions about careers. Write the answers.
Answer your partner's questions.

What do landscape gardeners do?

They design gardens and make them beautiful.

Career	What They Do
landscape gardener	design gardens and make them beautiful
orchestra conductor	lead musicians in a large group called an orchestra as they play music together
psychologist	
geologist	study the Earth, including rocks and minerals
forest ranger	
pharmacist	give people medicine and information about different kinds of medicine
carpenter	
baker	make bread, cakes, and other foods that are baked
reporter	
lawyer	work with clients
actor	

Communication Activity

Work with a partner: Student B uses this information and Student A uses the information on page 35.

Student B
Answer your partner's questions.
Ask questions about careers. Write the answers.

What do landscape gardeners do?

They design gardens and make them beautiful.

Career	What They Do
landscape gardener	design gardens and make them beautiful
orchestra conductor	
psychologist	study people's experiences and behavior
geologist	
forest ranger	work to protect and care for outdoor areas like parks
pharmacist	
carpenter	use wood to make objects and build structures
baker	
reporter	write news stories and articles
lawyer	
actor	act on stage and screen

Into the Future

A. Listen to the song. Write. Use words from the box.

In Our Future

Future fashions
_____
_____
_____

Future travel
_____
_____

Future viewing
_____

Homes
_____

cleaning robots
e-clothes
electric shoes
holographic TV
hypersonic plane
vacations on the moon
video jacket

B. Predict other things that might be in your future.

Food
_____
_____

Ways to communicate
_____
_____

C. Write a new verse.

For our future _____,

_____ may be the news.

I'll _____,

and you'll _____.

**A. What do they think life will be like in 2050?
Answer the questions with words and phrases from
the box. You will use one word more than once.**

1. What will cars of the future run on?

   _____

2. What will the air be like?

   _____

3. What will disappear from schools?

   _____

4. Where will students get information?

   _____

5. What will people's clothing be like?

   _____

6. Who will do most of the work?

   _____

7. Who will clean houses?

   _____

8. Who will help kids with homework?

   _____

9. What will people do with all their free time?

   _____

books
built-in computers
clean
the Internet
robots
solar power
vacations in space

What do Jason, Maria, and
Soo-Ji think life will be
like in 2050?

B. What do you think? Choose one and write about the future.

books	cars	free time	robots	schools

_____

_____

_____

_____

Cars **will** run on solar power.
We **won't** have jet-powered sneakers.

(I'm very sure about this.)

We **may** have robots to clean our houses.
We **might** have cars that can fly.
We **could** find life on Mars.

(I'm not very sure. It's possible.)

There **couldn't** be life on Pluto.

(This is impossible.)

3 **Write sentences. Give your opinion about life in 2050. Use *will, won't, may, might, could,* or *couldn't.***

1. travel in cars and planes driven by computers

   _____

2. travel underwater in cars

   _____

3. have GPS chips inside everything so we won't lose anything

   _____

4. have robots to cook, wash, and clean things

   _____

5. have robots in every home

   _____

6. have plastic "smart" cards to pay for everything we need

   _____

7. take vacations in outer space

   _____

8. listen to radio talk shows

   _____

9. eat pills instead of food

   _____

10. have 300-floor buildings

   _____

Do you think we will find life on another planet?
    We **might.**
    We **might** find life on another planet.
How will people travel in the future?
    People **may** have flying cars.

4 **A. Write questions. Use *Do you think*.**

1.   <u>Do you think we will find life on Mars?</u>
Yes, we will find life on Mars.

2. _____
Yes, we'll all have robots.

3. _____
No, we won't all have GPS chips in the future.

4. _____
We could fly in our own flying machines.

5. _____
I might get a holographic TV someday.

B. Write questions. Use *How will*.

1. _____
We might have robots to cook our meals in the year 2020.

2. _____
We may use plastic "smart" cards to pay for things.

3. _____
We could use the Internet to get all of our information.

4. _____
We might wear e-clothes.

5 Do the puzzle. Use the words that complete the sentences.

Across

1. Computer chips will tell ___ high in the sky where things are.
2. A ___ moves and works like a human but doesn't get tired!
3. Pictures will float in the air on ___ TVs.
4. All of our information will be downloaded from the ___.

What will life be like in the future?

Down

5. All cars will run on ___ power.
6. ___ planes will fly five times faster than the speed of sound.
7. ___ chips inside people, animals, and things will help to locate them.
8. Small, individual ___ systems may be used for travel in the air.
9. There won't be any air ___ because cars will run on power from the sun.
10. There may be life on other ___.

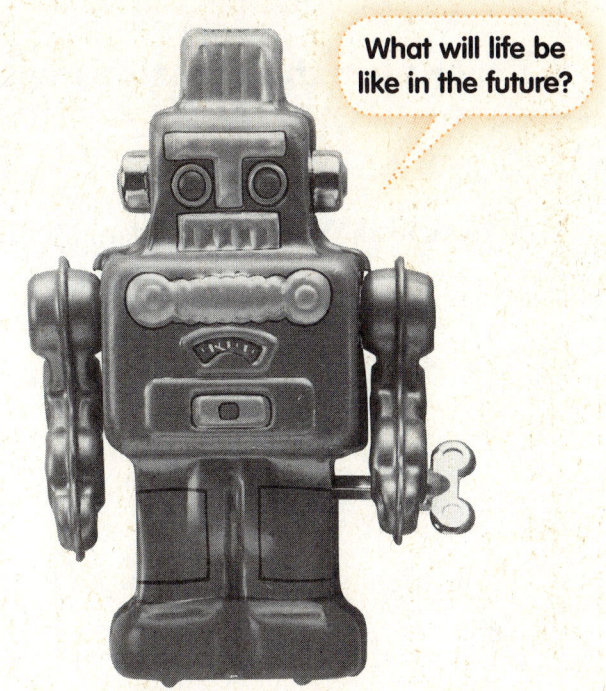

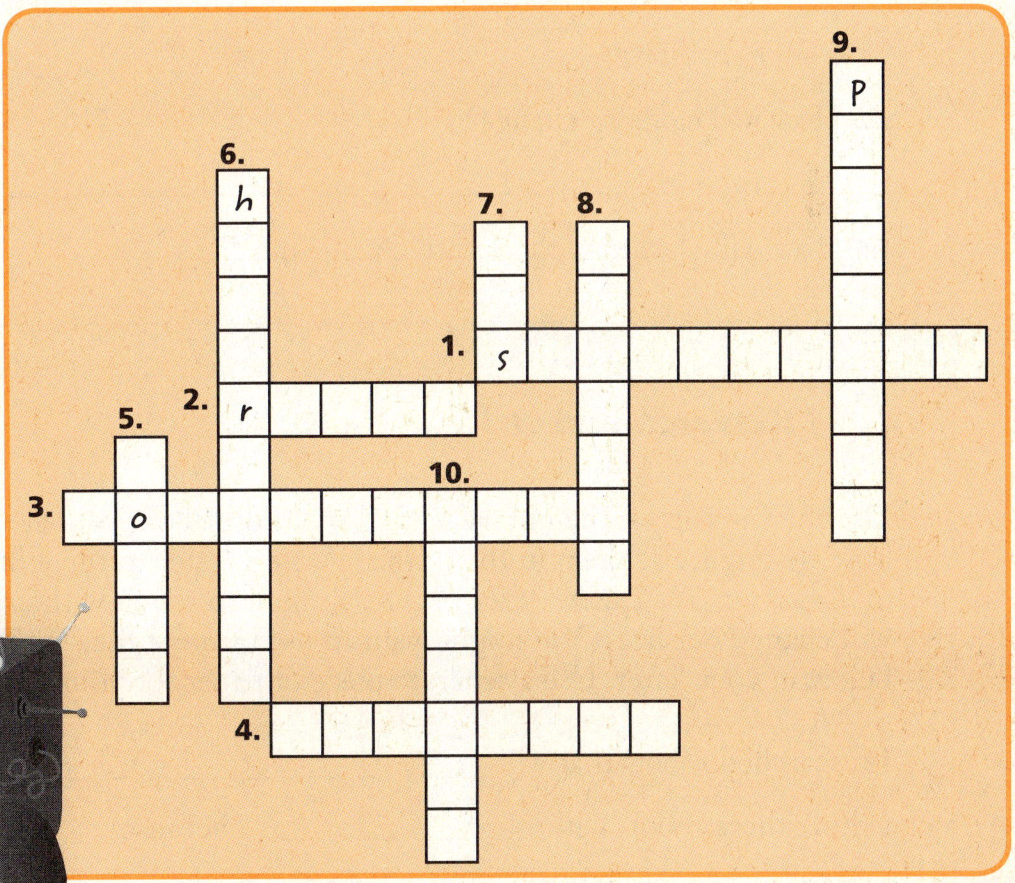
9.
p
6.
h
7.
8.
1.
s
2.
r
5.
10.
3.
o
4.

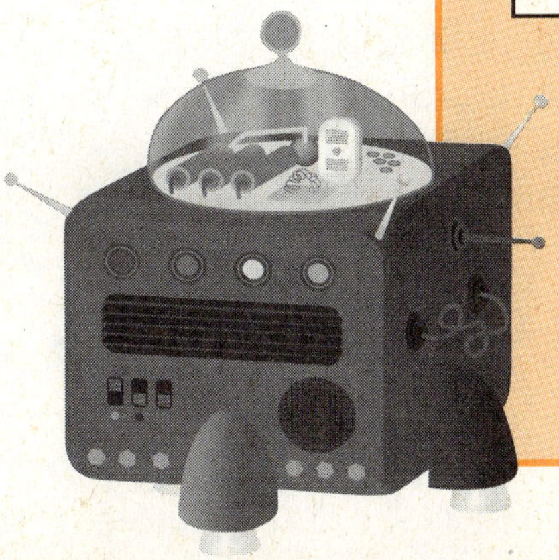

Read the magazine *Tomorrow: The E-Zine of the Future*.

6 **Answer the questions with complete sentences.**

Foods in Our Future

1. How will the population change in the future?

   _____

2. How will we have enough food?

   _____

Robots Win the World Cup!

3. How might soccer games of the future change?

   _____

4. How soon could this change happen?

   _____

Your Fashion Future

5. How will clothing change?

   _____

6. How will clothes of the future change our lives?

   _____

7 **Research and write.**

Use the Internet or the library to find out more about robots and how we might use them in the future. Write a letter to the editor of *Tomorrow: The E-Zine of the Future*. Be sure to tell how the robots will change our lives. You might want to use some of the sentences below in your letter. Use a separate piece of paper for your letter.

I researched robots that will _____.

I think these robots will _____ because _____.

8 **Listen to the predictions and circle.**

1. In 100 years, people **will / won't** live under the sea.

2. People **will / won't** live on the moon.

3. Cities **will / won't** be enclosed in plastic bubbles.

4. People **might / will** eat little food pills.

5. Life **could / couldn't** be as difficult under the sea as on the moon.

9 **A. What does the future hold? Use words from the box. Listen to the chant to check.**

Predictions

1. Way to travel   **a.** _____

2. Way to have more time at home   **a.** _____

3. Ways to communicate   **a.** _____

                            b. _____

4. Way to have fun   **a.** _____

> computer
> go beneath the sea
> jetpack
> videophone
> work there

B. Write some new lines for the chant.

I'd like to know what the future holds,

   but it seems so far away.

How will I get to my future _____—

   by _____ every day?

Or maybe _____ will _____,

   and I'll never _____.

I might _____ and _____ and _____

   by _____ and _____.

Or maybe I'll go _____

   to spend an exciting day.

I can't wait to see what the future brings,

   but it's still so far away!

Unit 4

43

Writing

Paragraph of Opinion

In a paragraph of opinion, you describe your point of view—how you feel or what you believe about a subject. You should state your opinion clearly in the first sentence of your paragraph, using a phrase such as *I believe, I think that*, or *in my opinion*. In the other sentences of your paragraph, you list facts, reasons, or examples that support your opinion. In your concluding sentence, you restate your opinion in different words.

Robots, Not Spaceships
by Maria Parson

I believe that robots, not spaceships, should be the focus of technological development in the future. First, robots are much less expensive to develop and build than spaceships. The cost of any spaceship is many millions of dollars more than the cost of the most sophisticated robot. **Second,** robots have useful applications on Earth right now. Even the robots we have now can work in dangerous conditions that humans cannot, such as extreme heat or cold. They can rescue people in collapsed mines, take apart bombs, work underwater, and help with delicate microscopic surgery. They are useful to society now in ways that spaceships are not. **Third,** robots can improve the life of the individual on a personal level. Robots can be developed to clean the house, do the shopping, cook, help with homework, play games, and keep track of the health of their human owners. No spaceship will ever affect the lives of individuals in such a way. **In conclusion, our lives will be better, sooner, when robots receive the attention, money, and time that spaceships do now.**

Writing Assignment

Using the following steps, you will write a paragraph of opinion about one of the topics below or another topic you are interested in. Remember that your topic sentence should state a belief, not a fact.

 Brainstorm Ideas

- Pick one of these topics or a topic of your own.
  - entertainment in the future
  - one world, one language
  - the disappearance of paper money
  - life on other planets
  - schools of the future
  - travel in the future

- State your belief in a clear topic sentence.
- Collect at least three facts, reasons, or examples to support your opinion.

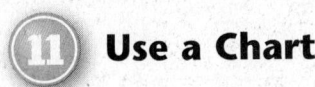 **Use a Chart**

A chart can help you put your facts in the order that you want to write about them. Include all of your facts. (The chart below is a sample, and does not contain all of the facts from the paragraph.)

Introduction	I believe that robots, not spaceships, should be the focus of technological development in the future.
Reason one	Robots are much less expensive to develop and build than spaceships.
Reason two	Robots have useful applications on Earth right now.
Reason three	Robots can improve the life of the individual on a personal level.
Conclusion	Our lives will be better, sooner, when robots receive the attention, money, and time that spaceships do now.

Use this chart to practice. Then make a complete chart on a piece of paper.

Introduction	
Reason one	
Reason two	
Reason three	
Conclusion	

┌─ To help you . . . ──────────────────────────────────────┐
│ **Expressions:** │
│ I believe   I think that   in conclusion   in my opinion │
└──┘

 **Write**

Use your chart to help you write your paragraph of opinion about a subject you are interested in. Write your paragraph on a separate piece of paper.

Review

13 **Write questions or answers about the future.**

1. Do you think scientists will work with genes to change living things, such as fruits, vegetables, and animals?

   _____

2. Do you think we'll have chocolate-flavored broccoli in the future?

   _____

3. _____

   We might have candy spaghetti. I'm not sure.

4. _____

   We will have faster and safer transportation.

5. Do you think we'll have cars that can fly or navigate underwater?

   _____

6. _____

   Some scientists think we all might have special GPS chips inside.

7. How will our free time be different?

   _____

8. _____

   We won't have money. We'll have "smart" cards to buy everything.

14 **Make predictions. Write. Use *may*, *might*, *will*, *won't*, or *could*.**

1. How will a robot help you in the future?

   _____

   _____

2. How will our homes be different?

   _____

   _____

Communication Activity

Work with a partner: Student A uses this information and Student B uses the information on page 48.

Student A
Ask questions about the future. Write the answers.
Answer your partner's questions.

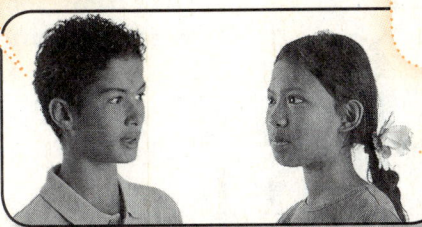

How will travel be different?

We'll have computer chips with all of our information. We won't have to carry passports, credit cards, money, or medical information.

What?	How will they (it) be different?
travel	• computer chips with all of our information • no need to carry passports, credit cards, money or medical information
homes	smaller
vacations	
cars	steer and brake themselves
pets	
apartment buildings	more floors with everything we need—stores, restaurants, and movies
clothes	
medical help	use a wireless monitor
work	
school	books replaced with Internet
emergencies	

Communication Activity

Work with a partner: Student B uses this information and Student A uses the information on page 47.

Student B
Answer your partner's questions.
Ask questions about the future. Write the answers.

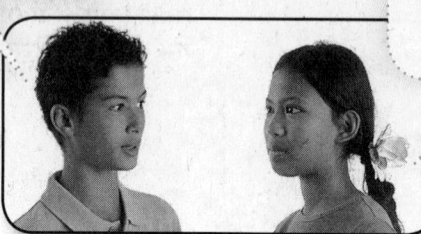

How will travel be different?

We'll have computer chips with all of our information. We won't have to carry passports, credit cards, money, or medical information.

What?	How will they (it) be different?
travel	• computer chips with all of our information • no need to carry passports, credit cards, money, or medical information
homes	
vacations	spaceships to the Moon and hypersonic planes to the other side of the Earth
cars	
pets	smaller
apartment buildings	
clothes	• adapt to changing temperatures • change colors • self-cleaning
medical help	
work	done by robots
school	
emergencies	medical information on plastic "smart" cards

5 Space

TRACK 15

1 A. Circle T for *true* or F for *false*. Then listen to the song and check.

House for Sale!

1. Mercury is burning hot.	T	F
2. Mercury is far from the sun.	T	F
3. Venus has a thick, hazy atmosphere.	T	F
4. It's sunny on Venus.	T	F
5. The atmosphere on Neptune is still and calm.	T	F
6. Pluto is large.	T	F

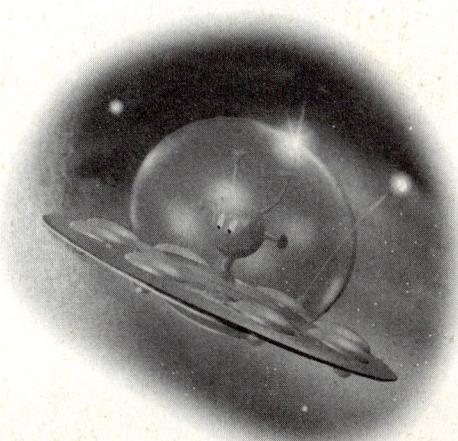

B. Which is the best planet to live on? Why?

_____

_____

_____

_____

Write complete questions or answers.

1. Which planet is closest to the sun?

   _____

2. _____

   Neptune is the farthest planet from the sun.

3. Which is the planet with the most moons?

   _____

4. _____

   Neptune is the windiest planet.

5. Which is the planet with the most English speakers?

   _____

6. _____

   The planet with the most rings is Saturn.

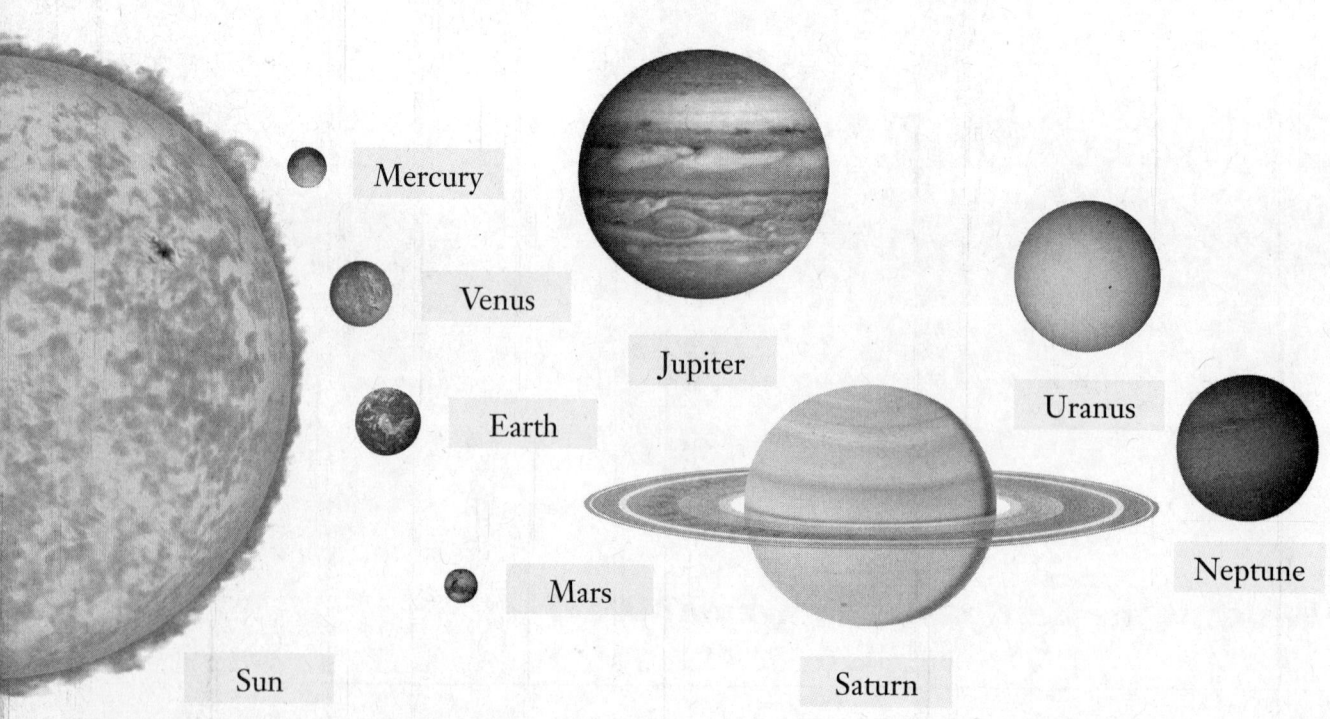

Mercury

Venus

Jupiter

Earth

Uranus

Mars

Neptune

Sun

Saturn

Real situation: I don't live on Mercury. I'm not very hot.
Unreal situation: If I lived on Mercury, I'd be very hot!

I'd = I would

3 **Is it real or unreal? Check the box.**

	Real	Unreal
1. I can use a telescope and look at the stars.	☐	☐
2. If I went to Jupiter's Great Red Spot, I'd get caught in a hurricane.	☐	☐
3. If you were a comet, you'd disappear after about 500 trips near the sun.	☐	☐
4. You can see a shooting star in the night sky.	☐	☐
5. If you lived on Neptune, you'd blow around in the windstorms.	☐	☐

> If I lived on Mercury, I'd be very close to the sun!

4 **Combine the sentences. Use *if* and *I'd*.**

1. I don't live on Venus. I don't cough in the thick atmosphere.

_____

2. I don't live on Jupiter. I don't see many moons at night.

_____

3. I'm not a supernova. I don't use more energy than the sun will ever use.

_____

4. I don't live on Neptune. I don't blow around like a feather.

_____

5. I don't live on Mars. I don't get caught in dust storms.

_____

6. I'm not a scientist. I don't study supernovas.

_____

7. I don't have a spaceship. I don't fly to Jupiter.

5 **Unscramble the sentences. Write the words in the correct order.**

1. 7 / traveled / would / 10 / to / they / If / to / the / them / Mars / months / take / trip

   _____

2. weigh / she / lived / Jupiter / 228 / she / on / would / pounds / If

   _____

3. years / If / on / would / lived / be / I / Mercury / 45 / old / I

   _____

4. Earth / on / year / would / If / 29½ / Saturn / we / years / be / lived / a / long

   _____

5. Neptune / around / like / blow / feather / If / a / I / windstorms / to / went / would / me

   _____

6 **Write. What would you take with you if you took the long trip to Mars?**

for fun: _If I went to Mars, I would take_

_____

_____

snacks: _____

clothes: _____

_____

7 **Use the chart and examples to write what your age and weight would be on other planets.**

Planet	Pull of gravity	Time It Takes to Revolve Around the Sun
Mercury	0.38	0.241 Earth years
Venus	0.91	0.615 Earth years
Mars	0.38	1.88 Earth years
Jupiter	2.36	11.9 Earth years
Saturn	0.92	29.4 Earth years
Uranus	0.89	83.7 Earth years
Neptune	1.12	163.7 Earth years

Example: I weigh 95 pounds on Earth. To find out what I would weigh on Mars, I multiply my weight times 0.38 (zero point thirty-eight). This is the pull of gravity compared to Earth. **95 pounds x 0.38 = 36 pounds**

Example: I am 11 years old on Earth. To find how old I would be on Venus, I divide my age by 0.615. This is the time it takes Venus to revolve around the Sun. **11 years old ÷ 0.615 = 17 years old**

1. On _____, I would be _____ years old.

2. On _____, I would weigh _____ pounds.

3. On _____, I would be _____ years old.

4. On _____, I would weigh _____ pounds.

 8 **Do the word search.**

comet	gravity
Mars	Neptune
Pluto	scientist
solar	supernova
universe	Venus

```
V T S P U C O M E T
Z G M G S U S X R Y
W V G V E N U S X N
U N I V E R S E H E
Y L S L T G U K Y P
U A O A B R P E D T
F G E G N A E R P U
C V J S N V R D J N
L R T O A I N I C E
B M P L U T O R I J
D A K A N Y V G K U
R R Q R D O A I C P
A S C I E N T I S T
```

Read *Out There* magazine.

9 **Check *True* or *False*.**

Hubble Fact File

	True	False
1. The Hubble Telescope is named after astronomer Edwin P. Hubble.	☐	☐
2. The body of the Hubble is about the size of a basketball.	☐	☐
3. The telescope tube is as tall as a three-story building.	☐	☐
4. In space, the telescope weighs 25,000 pounds (11,339 kg), but it weighs nothing on Earth.	☐	☐

Ask Dan the Science Man

	True	False
5. Looking directly at the sun during a solar eclipse can cause blindness.	☐	☐
6. The retina of the eye feels pain.	☐	☐
7. Your eye has a lens just like a camera.	☐	☐

10 **Research and write.**

Find out about a recent space mission. Gather information at the library or on the Internet. Take notes below. Write a paragraph about it. Use a separate piece of paper. Include this information:

1. **What:** What country sponsored the mission?
2. **Who:** Who were the astronauts?
3. **Where:** Where did the spacecraft travel?
4. **When:** When was the mission?
5. **How:** How will the mission help us understand space better?

_____

_____

_____

_____

_____

11 Listen and complete the chart.

Asteroids

Asteroids are small objects made of:

They are sometimes called:

Ceres, the largest known asteroid, has a diameter of:

Most asteroids are between the planets:

One theory says that asteroids were originally pieces of:

Another theory says asteroids were pieces that never:

An asteroid that strikes Earth is called a:

One example of impact is found in:

12 Choose and write rhyming words from the box. Then listen to the chant and check.

be	bright
face	galaxy
meteorite	night
place	see
space	

Through the Lens

If I had a giant telescope,

this is what I'd _____—

millions of shining stars

in a faraway _____.

I'd see a comet streaking by

with its tail so _____,

or a mass of rock and iron

that could be a _____.

So if I had a telescope,

I'd be in just one _____—

with my eye pressed to the lens

exploring outer _____.

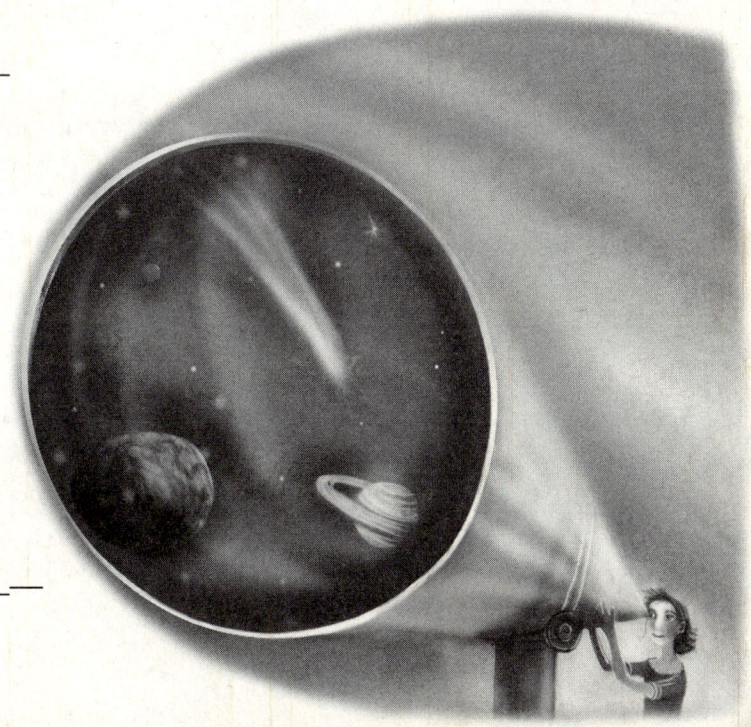

Unit 5

55

Writing

Sentence Variety in a Paragraph

When you write a paragraph, you should use different kinds of sentences. To make your writing more interesting, you can use some short sentences. You can also use some longer sentences with *and*, *or*, or *but*. Then, for more variety, you can include some sentences with *if* clauses or other clauses.

Which paragraph is more interesting? Why?

Paragraph One

    I would like to visit Mars, the Red Planet. I would like to see its red dust. I would like to see the sand. My shoes would make footprints in it. I would wear my helmet to protect my eyes from the sand. I would protect myself from the dust. I would take samples of the dust and sand. I would look for water and signs of life. I would follow my footprints back to my spaceship. I would go back home. I would show my souvenirs to my friends and family.

Paragraph Two

    If I could visit any planet in our solar system, I would visit Mars. Because Mars looks red from here on Earth, we call it the Red Planet. But is it really red? I'd love to find out! After my landing, I imagine I would see mountains, valleys, huge rocks, sand, and dust. In my protective suit, I would leave my spaceship and I would carefully take samples from the ground. Then I'd look for signs of water, because scientists believe that water is a condition for life. After I finished my explorations, I would follow my footprints back to my spaceship. Then I would go back home to show my souvenirs to my friends and family.

Writing Assignment

Using the following steps, you will write a paragraph about an adventure you would like to have in space. Remember to include interesting details and different types of sentences.

 Brainstorm Ideas

- Pick one of these topics or a topic of your own. What would you see? What would you do?
    - explore a black hole   - follow a comet
    - go to the sun   - live on the International Space Station
    - see the Hubble Space Telescope   - visit a planet

Use Different Kinds of Sentences

After you know what you want to say, you can change some of your sentences so that they are not all the same.

Information you want to say:
The fourth planet is named Mars. Mars is often called the Red Planet. Mars looks red from here on Earth.

Changes you can make:

compound sentence with *but* or *and*
• The fourth planet is named Mars, but it is often called the Red Planet.   • Some people call the fourth planet Mars, and others call it the Red Planet.

complex sentence with *because*
• Because Mars looks red from here on Earth, we call it the Red Planet.   • Mars is called the Red Planet because it looks red from here on Earth.   • The fourth planet, Mars, is also called the Red Planet because it looks red from here on Earth.

Practice changing the sentences below in different ways. Use a separate piece of paper.

Information you want to say:
The fifth planet is named Jupiter. Jupiter is named after the king of the ancient Roman gods. Jupiter is the biggest planet in our solar system.

 Write

Write down the information you want to include in your paragraph. Practice saying the information in different ways. When you have a good variety of sentence types, write your paragraph on a separate piece of paper.

To help you . . .

Editing Tip:
When you finish your paragraph, read it aloud to a friend. Is your paragraph clear? Does it include interesting details? Does it have a variety of sentence types? Ask your friend. Make changes if necessary.

Review

 16 **Write sentences with *if* and *would*.**

1. I did not visit Mars. It did not take me 7 to 10 months to get there.

   If I visited Mars, it would take me 7 to 10 months to get there.

2. I am not a space mechanic. I don't walk 600 kilometers above Earth to fix something.

   _____

3. They did not look directly at a solar eclipse. They have not become blind.

   _____

4. The Hubble telescope is not on Earth. It does not weigh 25,000 pounds.

   _____

5. I don't live on Neptune. I am not very cold.

   _____

6. I don't live on Neptune. I don't blow around in the windstorms.

   _____

17 **Complete the questions or answers. Write complete sentences.**

1. What would happen if you _____?
   (go to the Great Red Spot)

   I'd be caught in a hurricane that has already lasted for 300 years!

2. What would happen if you lived on Neptune?

   _____
   (blow around in the windstorms)

3. What would happen if you _____?
   (live on Venus)

   I'd cough in the cloudy, thick, and hazy atmosphere.

4. What would it be like if you lived on Neptune?

   _____
   (dark and cold)

5. What would happen if you _____?
   (fall into a black hole)

   I'd stretch out like spaghetti and disappear.

Communication Activity

Work with a partner: Student A uses this information and Student B uses the information on page 60.

Student A

Ask questions about the planets. Write the answers.
Answer your partner's questions.

If I lived on Mars, how long would a year be?

A year would last 687 Earth days.

Which planet? What do I want to know?	Answer
Mars: length of a year	687 Earth days
Venus: how hot?	900° F (482° C)
Mercury: my age	
Mars: my weight	36 pounds (if you weigh 95 pounds on Earth)
Neptune: how cold?	
Neptune: distance from the sun	2,793 billion miles (4,495 billion kilometers)
Jupiter: number of moons	
Mars: travel time	7 to 10 months from Earth to Mars
Mars: my age	
Jupiter: my weight	224 pounds (if you weigh 95 pounds on Earth)
Saturn: length of a day	

Communication Activity

Work with a partner: Student B uses this information and Student A turns to page 59.

Student B
Answer your partner's questions.
Ask questions about the planets. Write the answers.

If I lived on Mars, how long would a year be?

A year would last 687 Earth days.

Which planet? What do I want to know?	Answer
Mars: length of a year	687 Earth days
Venus: how hot?	
Mercury: my age	46 years (if you're 11 on Earth)
Mars: my weight	
Neptune: how cold?	–346° F (–210°C)
Neptune: distance from the sun	
Jupiter: number of moons	63
Mars: travel time	
Mars: my age	about 6 years old (if you're 11 on Earth)
Jupiter: my weight	
Saturn: length of a day	10 hours, 40 minutes

6 Adventures

TRACK 18

1 **A. Write. Use words from the box. Then listen to the song and check.**

biked
crossed
gone
jumped
paddled
wore

Top This!

1. He's already _____ up a mountain.

2. He's already _____ with a parachute

   from an airplane— _____ a diving suit.

3. He's _____ rapids and he _____ really fast.

4. He hasn't _____ to space yet.

B. Complete the chart. Check. Add more activities.

Have you ever . . . ?	I've already . . .	I haven't yet . . .	I'm planning to . . .
1. ridden a mountain bike			
2. gone in an airplane			
3. jumped with a parachute			
4. crossed rapids			
5. traveled in space			
6.			
7.			
8.			

C. Write sentences about what you've already done and not done yet.

1. *I've already gone in an airplane.*

2. _____

3. _____

4. _____

Unit 6

61

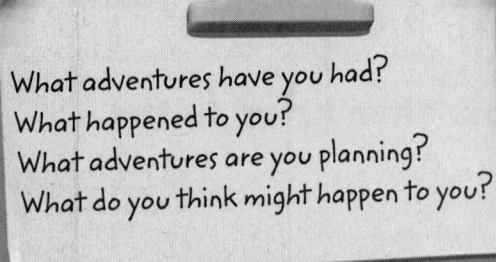

What adventures have you had?
What happened to you?
What adventures are you planning?
What do you think might happen to you?

I've gone skydiving once. The wind blew me into a lake.

Have you ever **parachuted** from a plane?
Would you ever **parachute** from a plane?

A. Ask and write the names.

What?	Have you ever . . . ?	Would you ever . . . ? Yes	No
climb a mountain	Maria	Manuel, Juan	Marta
go white-water rafting			
go horseback riding			
parachute from a plane			
ride a hot-air balloon			
go sledding in a snowstorm			
explore underwater caves			

B. Interview one person from the second column of your chart. Write about the adventure.

Who and what: _____

_____

Where and when: _____

_____

C. Interview one person from the third column of your chart. Write.

Who and what: _____

_____

Why or why not: _____

_____

D. How about you? Choose and write.

What: _____

_____

Where and when / Why or why not: _____

_____

Have Franz and Maria **climbed** Mount McKinley yet?
Yes, they already **have**. They climbed it last month.
No, they **haven't**. They're planning to do it next month.

4 **Complete the questions. Use the correct form of the verb.**

1. Yoko: _Have you windsurfed_ yet? (windsurf)
   Iris: No, I haven't. I'm planning to go windsurfing next summer.

2. Kate: _____ in an airplane yet? (travel)
   Tom: Yes, I already went on a plane to see my grandmother in Brazil.

3. Eric: _____ a mountain bike yet? (ride)
   Diana: Yes, I already have. I rode a mountain bike on my vacation last week.

4. Ilhan: _____ horseback riding yet? (go)
   Mario: Yes, I have. And I've already fallen off three times!

Grammar

Would they ever **parachute** from a plane?   **Would** they ever **go** scuba diving?
Yes, they **would**.   No, they **wouldn't**.

5 **Use the information from the chart. Answer in complete sentences.**

Who?	Likes	Dislikes
Mario	running fast	being in high places
Barbara	reading about space adventures	being underwater
Julio	mountain climbing	flying in airplanes

1. Would Mario ever go mountain climbing? Why or why not?

   _____

2. Would Barbara ever try scuba diving? Why or why not?

   _____

3. Would Barbara ever travel into space? Why or why not?

   _____

4. Would Julio ever climb Mount Everest? Why or why not?

   _____

Look at the picture clues. Complete the question *Have you ever . . . ?* **Write the missing words in the puzzle. One is done for you.**

11.

1. <u>s</u> <u>a</u> <u>i</u> <u>l</u> <u>e</u> <u>d</u>

2. __ __ __ __ __

3. __ __ __ __ __ __ __ __ __

4. __ __ __ __

5. __ __ __ __ __ __ __ __

6. __ __ __ __ __ __ __

7. <u>j</u> __ __ __ __

8. <u>e</u> __ __ __ __ __ __

9. __ __ __ __ __

10. __ __ __ __ __

Write the word formed by the letters in the boxes.

_____

Read *Adventure Magazine.*

 Answer the questions.

A Rumble in the Jungle

1. Have you ever gone on a canopy adventure tour?

_____

2. If you've been on a canopy tour, what did you see?

_____

3. If you haven't been on a canopy tour, would you ever go? Why or why not?

_____

4. Have you ever been bungee jumping?

_____

5. If you have, what was it like?

_____

6. Would you ever do it again? Why or why not?

_____

7. If you haven't bungee jumped, would you ever try it? Why or why not?

_____

8 **Research and write.**

A. Use the Internet or the library to find information about an exciting adventure you would like to try. You may want to research backpacking and hiking or a high-rope course.

B. Write a paragraph about the adventure. Tell where you would go on the adventure and what special training and equipment you would need. Use a separate piece of paper.

TRACK 19

9 **Listen. Check the things you can do on an adventure vacation in Chile.**

_____ 1. You can ride horses in Torres del Paine National Park in Chile.

_____ 2. You can see typical plants and animals.

_____ 3. You can fish for trout in many of the rivers.

_____ 4. You can hike through ancient forests of palm trees.

_____ 5. You can walk along the black sand by Grey Glacier Lake.

_____ 6. You can see chunks of glacier ice fall into the water.

_____ 7. You can photograph condors, *guanaco*, and *criollos*.

_____ 8. You can take hot showers every day after riding horses for hours.

TRACK 20

10 **Complete the chant questions with rhyming words from the box. Listen to check. Then write rhyming answers that begin with *Yes*. Choose words from the box.**

cave   survive   lump   wave   call   dive   save   Mike
ball   jump   Dave   bike   five   hike   pump   wall

Adventures?

Would you ever scale a _____?

No, I wouldn't. I might fall.   *Yes,* <u>I would. I'd have a ball!</u>

Would you ever bungee _____?

No way! I'm sure I'd get a bump.   *Yes,* _____

Would you ever scuba _____?

No, I'd rather stay alive.   *Yes,* _____

Would you ever explore a _____?

No, not me. I'm not that brave.   *Yes,* _____

Would you ever mountain _____?

No, that's something I don't like.   *Yes,* _____

Writing

Personal Narrative

When you write a personal narrative, you tell a story about an experience in your life. You can use time words (*first*, *after that*, *next*, *then*, *finally*) to show when things happened and in what order they happened. These words can also be used to guide your reader from one paragraph to another.

My Trip to Disney World
by Tony Hernandez

Have you ever had a dream come true? I have. When I was seven years old, I went to Disney World with my family. It was a fantastic experience. There was so much to see, and so many rides to go on. We wanted to experience everything, but we knew we only had two days. We had to plan our time very carefully.

The first day, we explored the different theme parks. We went on an exciting canoe trip down some really fast rapids. We explored a very dark, cold cave. We even visited a campsite and roasted marshmallows. After that, we waited until dark to see the famous Disney parade. There were so many clowns! The music, colors, and lights were awesome!

The next day, we bought tickets for our favorite rides. We went on the *Tea Cup* and *It's a Small World* in the morning. We had so much fun! Then we went on *Magic Mountain* in the afternoon. That was the fastest ride we went on. It was a little scary, and it wasn't very smart of us to go on that ride right after lunch!

Finally, it was time to go home. We bought some souvenirs in the gift shop, waved goodbye to Mickey and Minnie Mouse, and got into our car. My sister and I cried all the way home because our wonderful trip was over. It was the best family adventure that I have ever had!

Writing Assignment

Using the following steps, you will write a personal narrative about an adventurous experience in your life.

Brainstorm Ideas

- Choose an adventure you had or a trip you went on.
- Think about the different things that happened. Decide which events you are going to write about.
- Think about details such as the time, place, people, and events.
- How did you feel during and after the experience?

12 Use a Sequence Chart

Writing notes in a sequence chart can help you organize your ideas.

Paragraph 1: time and place [Where did you go?/What did you do?]	• visited Disney World • when I was 7 years old
Paragraph 2: *First, . . .*	• explored theme park 1. went on a canoe trip 2. explored a cave 3. visited a campsite 4. saw a parade
Paragraph 3: *Next/Then/After that . . .*	• went on rides 1. Tea Cup 2. It's a Small World 3. Magic Mountain
Paragraph 4: *Finally, . . .*	• bought souvenirs • said goodbye to Mickey and Minnie Mouse • cried all the way home

Use this chart to practice. Make your own chart on a separate piece of paper.

Paragraph 1: time and place	
Paragraph 2: *First, . . .*	1. 2. 3.
Paragraph 3: *Next/Then/After that, . . .*	1. 2. 3.
Paragraph 4: *Finally, . . .*	1. 2.

To help you . . .

Action Words:

bike	climb	dive	explore	fall	go	jump	race
rescue	run	sail	ski	skydive	surf	swim	visit

13 Write

Use your sequence chart to help you write a personal narrative about an adventure you have experienced. Write your narrative on a separate piece of paper.

Review

14 **Answer the questions. Use *yet* or *already*.**

1. Has Yoko climbed Mount Everest yet?

   No, _she hasn't climbed it yet. She's planning to climb it next year._
   (next year)

2. Have Lee and Kim gone on a canopy tour of the rain forest yet?

   No, _____
   (next week)

3. Has Anna gone white-water rafting yet?

   Yes, _____
   (last month)

4. Has Tomo ridden on an elephant yet?

   Yes, _____
   (last week)

5. Has Yoshiko gone bungee jumping yet?

   No, _____
   (next Friday)

6. Has Jim skied in a snowstorm yet?

   Yes, _____
   (last Saturday)

15 **Write questions about adventures. Then write your answers.**

1. Would you ever _____?

   _____

2. Would you ever _____?

   _____

3. Would you ever _____?

   _____

Communication Activity

Work with a partner: Student A uses this information and Student B uses the information on page 72.

Student A
Ask questions about the adventures. Write the answers.
Answer your partner's questions.

Has Maria gone sledding down Horror Hill yet?

Yes, she already has. She went sledding down Horror Hill yesterday!

Who?	What?	Yes/No	When?
Maria	sledding down Horror Hill	yes	yesterday
José	white-water rafting	no	next week
Paul and Paula	bungee jumping		
Lucy	exploring caves	no	in three hours
Steven	hiking up Mount Fuji		
Melissa	racing in the Iditarod	yes	2005
Rhea	scuba diving		
Robert	windsurfing	no	tomorrow
Emma	horseback riding		
Adam	parachuting from a plane	no	next month
Gina	mountain biking		

Communication Activity

Work with a partner: Student B uses this information and Student A uses the information on page 71.

Student B
Answer your partner's questions.
Ask questions about the adventures. Write the answers.

Has Maria gone sledding down Horror Hill yet?

Yes, she already has. She went sledding down Horror Hill yesterday!

Who?	What?	Yes/No	When?
Maria	sledding down Horror Hill	yes	yesterday
José	white-water rafting		
Paul and Paula	bungee jumping	yes	last month
Lucy	exploring caves		
Steven	hiking up Mount Fuji	no	next year
Melissa	racing in the Iditarod		
Rhea	scuba diving	yes	last summer
Robert	windsurfing		
Emma	horseback riding	yes	last week
Adam	parachuting from a plane		
Gina	mountain biking	yes	last fall

7 A World of Records

A. Listen to the song. Circle T for *true* or F for *false*.

Ask the Expert

1. The Cambodian alphabet has the most letters of any alphabet.   T   F

2. Hollywood makes the most movies.   T   F

3. Pelé scored the most soccer goals of any professional player.   T   F

4. Andy Green flew the fastest in a plane.   T   F

5. Venezuela has the world's smallest waterfall.   T   F

6. The tallest person on record was Robert Wadlow.   T   F

7. Jupiter has the most moons of all, a total of 42.   T   F

8. A camel has the most eyelids of any animal— 3 eyelids on each eye.   T   F

9. The smallest town on record is the town of Valley Park, Oklahoma.   T   F

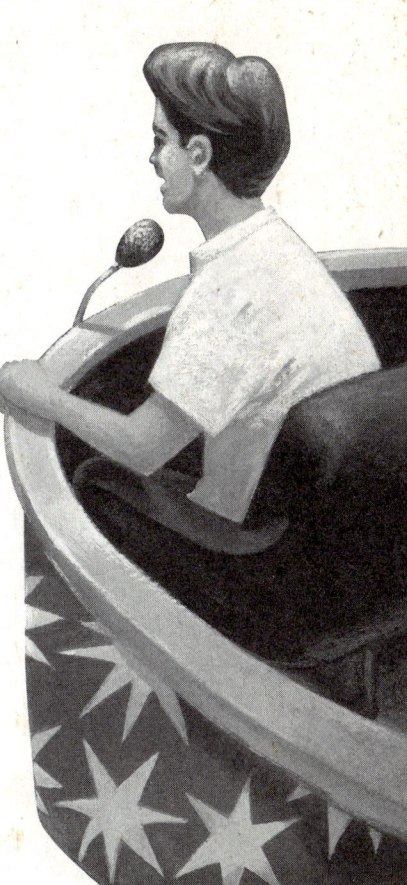

B. Write new sentences that make the false items in Part A true.

_____

_____

_____

_____

_____

2 **Read *Animal Records* again. Write the words from the box in the correct columns. Some words may go in more than one column.**

big	centimeters		fast	feet	heavy
inches	kilometers per hour		long	meters	miles per hour
slow	tall		tons	weigh	

Height	Length	Speed	Weight

3 **Match the words and phrases on the left with the phrases on the right. Write the letter.**

_____ 1. sailfish

_____ 2. speed of a sailfish

_____ 3. sea horse

_____ 4. speed of a sea horse

_____ 5. blue whale

_____ 6. weight of a blue whale

_____ 7. black mamba

_____ 8. Goliath birdeater

_____ 9. length of the biggest spider

_____ 10. giraffe

_____ 11. height of a giraffe

_____ 12. koala

a. 143 tons

b. world's deadliest snake

c. 11 inches

d. biggest spider

e. world's fastest fish

f. 68 miles per hour

g. heaviest sea animal

h. .001 miles per hour

i. world's slowest fish

j. sleepiest animal

k. 18 feet tall

l. tallest animal

Grammar

Adjectives: Comparing two things
old: I am old**er than** David.
friendly: Susan is friend**lier than** Karen.
patient: My mother is **less patient than** my father.
interesting: English is **more interesting than** math.

Adjectives: Comparing three or more things
old: I am **the oldest** boy in my class.
friendly: Susan is **the friendliest** girl in my class.
patient: My math teacher is **the least patient** person I know.
interesting: Action movies are **the most interesting** movies.

Matterhorn: 14,692 feet
(4,478 m)

4 **Complete the sentences with the correct forms.**

1. Mount Grosvenor in China is 21,190 feet (6,459 m) high. The Matterhorn, on the border between Switzerland and Italy, is 14,692 feet (4,478 m) high. Mount

   Grosvenor is _____ the Matterhorn. (high)

2. Today is _____ yesterday. It might rain today. (cloudy)

3. I think a vacation in the mountains is _____ a vacation at the beach. You always do the same kinds of things at the beach. (boring)

4. The world's _____ man was Robert Wadlow. (tall)

5. Bill is _____ student in my class. Everyone likes him because he is so friendly. (popular)

6. Last night's soccer game was _____ of the year. I almost fell asleep! (exciting)

Grammar

More/fewer + noun: Comparing two things
more + noun: Edward has **more video games than** George does.
fewer + noun: I have **fewer cousins than** you do.

The most/fewest + noun: Comparing three or more things
The most + noun: Mark has **the most sports medals** of anyone in school.
The fewest + noun: Jennifer had **the fewest mistakes** of all on the test.

5 **Complete the sentences with *more*, *fewer*, *the most*, or *the fewest*.**

1. The Hawaiian alphabet has 14 letters. It has _____ letters than Rotokas, which has 11 letters.

2. The Tokyo subway has about 3 billion riders a year. The New York City subway has about 2 billion riders a year. The New York City subway has _____ riders than the Tokyo subway.

3. More people speak Mandarin Chinese as a native language than any other language. Mandarin Chinese has about 500 million _____ native speakers than English does.

4. Gary Duschl collected _____ gum wrappers to make the longest chain. His chain has more than 1 million wrappers and measures over 50,000 feet (15,240 m) long.

5. The Spanish word with _____ letters is *electroencefalografistas*. It has 24 letters and is a type of medical worker.

6. Aswan, Egypt, gets only .02 inches (.5 mm) of rain a year. It gets _____ inches of rain of any inhabited city.

6 **Read the chart and write sentences. Use *more than/ the most* or *fewer than/the fewest* + a noun.**

China		Peru		Vatican City	
people:	1.3 billion	people:	29,180,899	people:	890
area:	3,705,386 sq mi (9,596,960 sq km)	area:	496,223 sq mi (1,285,220 sq km)	area:	0.17 sq mi (0.44 sq km)
languages:	Chinese	languages:	Spanish, Quechua, Aymara	language:	Italian

1. _____

_____

2. _____

_____

3. _____

_____

7 Write sentences about some records in your family. Use *more than/the most* or *fewer than/the fewest* + a noun. Use ideas from the box and some ideas of your own.

CDs	chores
comic books	desserts
e-mails	freckles
hobbies	phone calls
sneakers	stuffed animals
toys	video games

1. _____

2. _____

3. _____

4. _____

5. _____

6. _____

8 Do the puzzle.

Across

1. an alphabet with 74 letters
2. the planet with more than 60 moons
3. the fastest fish in the world
4. the country that exports the most rice in a year

Down

5. the heaviest sea animal
6. Robert ___, the world's tallest person
7. the country with the highest waterfall
8. the language with more than 1 billion speakers

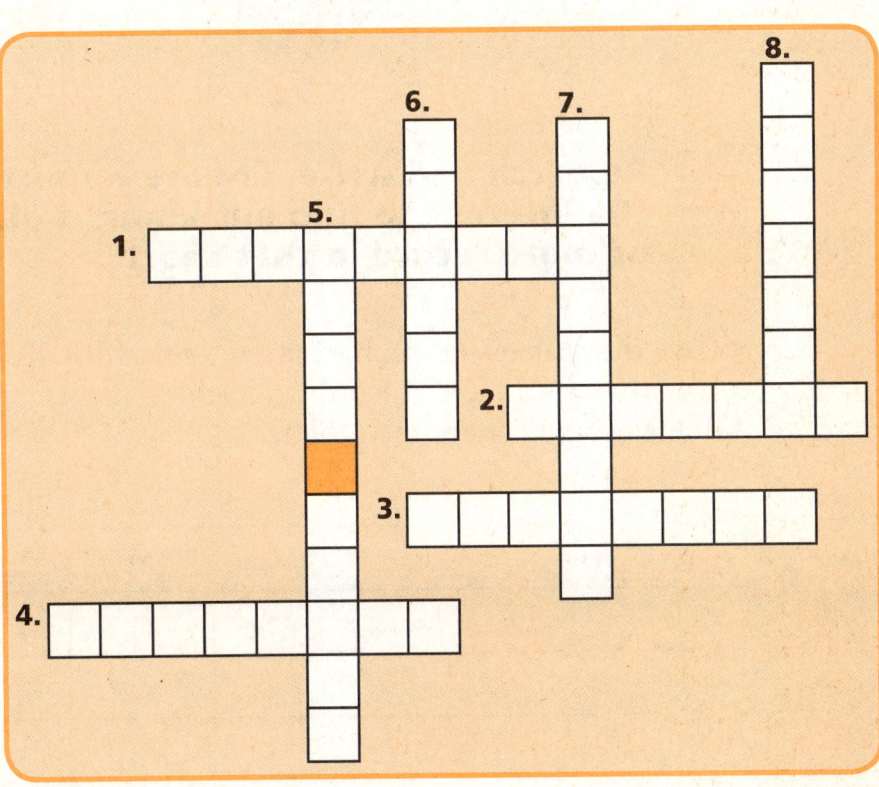

Read *Remarkable Records Magazine*.

9 **Write the name of the person, place, or thing on each award.**

Award for the most
Olympic medals

_____
(name)

Award for the ride with the
most thrills

_____
(name)

Award for the most goals in
World Cup history

_____
(name)

Award for the most points in
a basketball career

_____
(name)

10 **Research and write. Choose a sport. Use the library and the Internet to find out about a player that holds one or more record in that sport.**

- Give the athlete's name, birthplace, age, and sport.
- Describe the athlete's records and achievements.
- Tell why you admire this athlete.

_____

_____

_____

_____

_____

_____

Design an award or trophy for
your athlete.

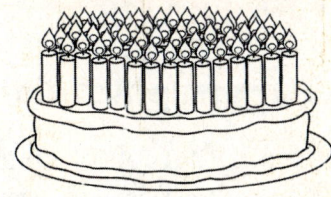

TRACK 22

11 **Listen and answer the questions.**

1. What are some examples of Paul Sahli's records?

   _____

2. What are some examples of Jim Mouth's records?

   _____

3. What are some examples of Ashrita Furman's records?

   _____

4. Why is it important to look at more than one source for information?

   _____

TRACK 23

12 **Complete the sentences. Use words from the box. Then listen to the chant and check your answers.**

| best |
| deepest |
| fewest |
| first |
| most |

Daydream Record

1. He wants to win _____ place.

2. He wants to dive in the _____ ocean.

3. He wants to spend the _____ time in space.

4. He wants to get the _____ test score in school.

5. He wants to make the _____ mistakes.

13 **Write. Describe a record you would like to set and tell what you would do.**

_____
(title)

_____

_____

_____

_____

_____

Unit 7

Writing

Paragraph of Comparison

In a paragraph of comparison, you describe how two things, people, or ideas in the same category are similar. You can use adjectives to describe similarities, and you can use words and expressions such as *also*, *as well as*, *both*, *each of*, *in the same way*, *like*, and *too*.

My Two Best Friends
by Marcia Wellington

Karen and Angie are my two best friends at school. They are similar in several ways. **Both** have brown eyes and dark, wavy hair. They even style their hair **in the same way** and have the same taste in clothes. Karen is as friendly as Angie, and as energetic as she is, **too**. **Like** Karen, Angie is hardworking and smart. They both like math more than their other subjects in school. **Each of** them, in different years, has won the school math competition. In fact, Angie, **as well as** Karen, wants to be a math teacher one day. Both of my friends have similar after-school interests. For example, they enjoy playing sports. Angie is a good soccer player, and Karen is, too. Both like hiking and swimming as well. And, like me, they **also** love listening to music, reading, and shopping. I think I'm lucky to have such wonderful friends.

Writing Assignment

Using the following steps, you will write a paragraph comparing two things, people, or ideas that interest you.

 ## Brainstorm Ideas

- Pick one of these topics or a topic of your own.
  - two family members
  - two friends
  - two record-breakers
  - two similar animals
  - two sports
  - two vacations

- What do they have in common? What is interesting about them?

 ## Use a Venn Diagram

A Venn diagram can help you compare two items. The area where both circles meet clearly shows similarities. These are the details you use in a comparison. In the example that follows on the next page, you would not use the other details. These show how the friends are different.

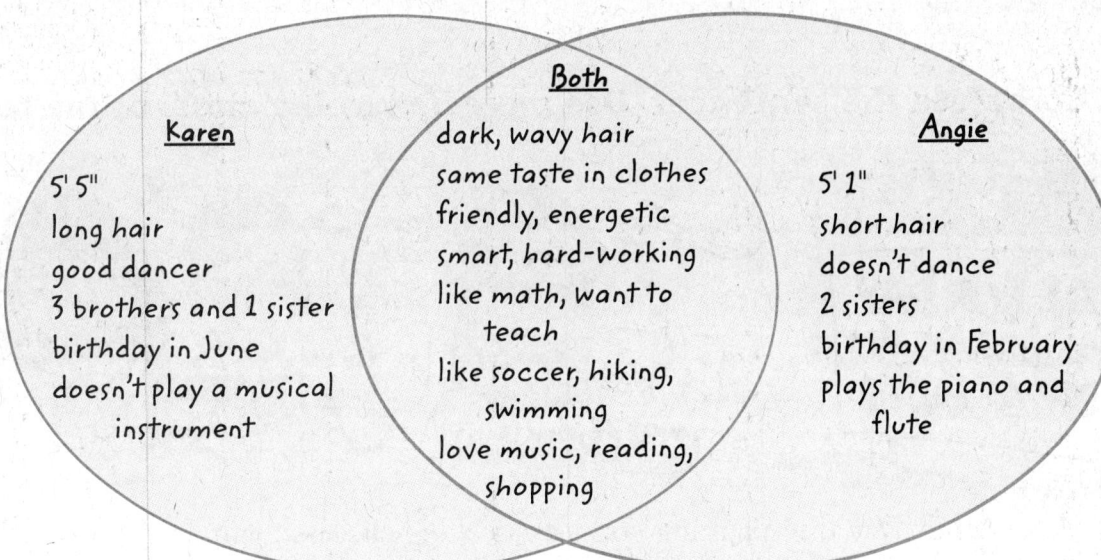

Karen

5' 5"
long hair
good dancer
3 brothers and 1 sister
birthday in June
doesn't play a musical
    instrument

Both

dark, wavy hair
same taste in clothes
friendly, energetic
smart, hard-working
like math, want to
    teach
like soccer, hiking,
    swimming
love music, reading,
    shopping

Angie

5' 1"
short hair
doesn't dance
2 sisters
birthday in February
plays the piano and
    flute

Complete the Venn diagram with your ideas for your paragraph.

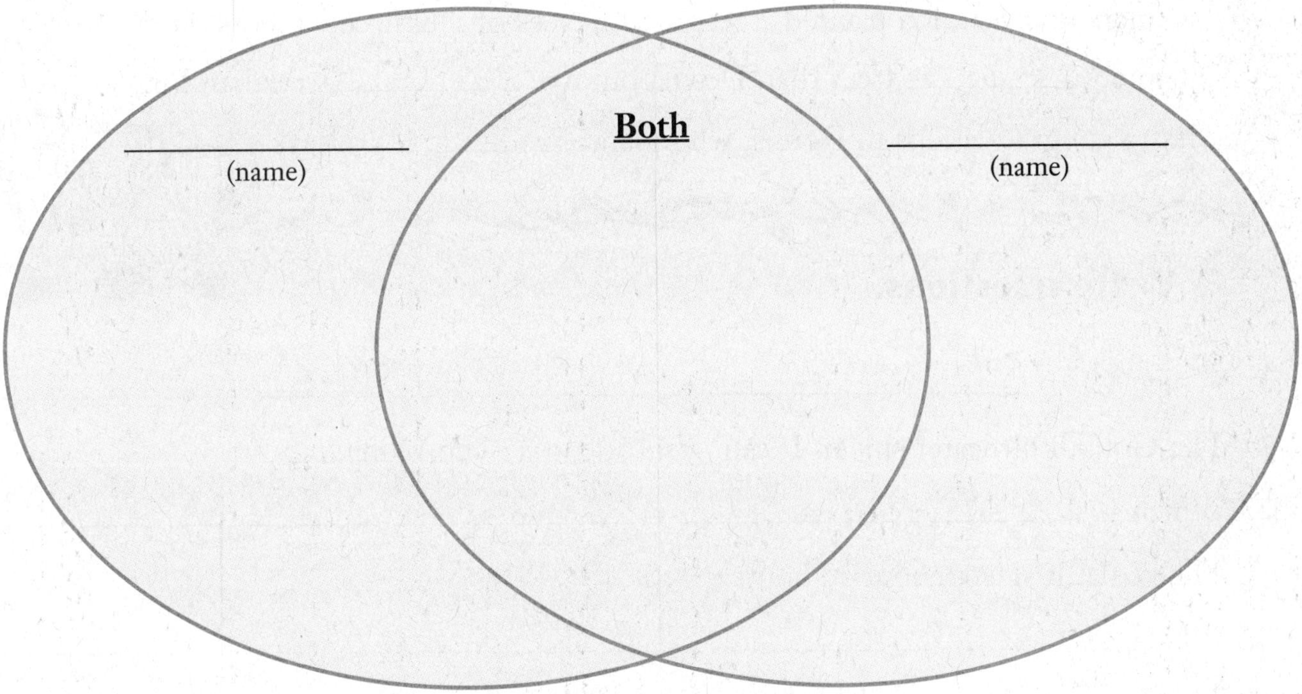

_____
(name)

Both

_____
(name)

┌─ To help you . . . ───┐
│ **Transition Words:**   │
│ also   and   as well as   both   each of   in the same way   like   too │
└──┘

16 Write

Use your Venn diagram to help you write a paragraph of comparison. Write your
paragraph on a separate piece of paper.

Review

17 **Complete the sentences. Use *more, fewer, the most,* or *the fewest*.**

Our Arbor Day tree-planting contest was a big success. Sam, last year's winner, planted eleven new trees, three _____ trees than this year's winner. Donna, this year's top winner, planted _____ new trees than any other winner in the past. Jack and Pia were second- and third-place winners this year. Pia planted _____ trees of the three winners. Jack planted _____ trees than Donna but one _____ tree than Pia. Extra congratulations to Donna, who planted _____ trees!

18 **Write questions.**

1. Which _____

   The Goliath birdeater spider. It can be 11 inches (28 cm) long.

2. Which _____

   The koala. It sleeps about 20 hours a day.

3. Which _____

   The sea horse. It moves about .001 mile (.002 km) per hour.

4. Which _____

   Strahov Stadium in the Czech Republic. It holds about 220,000 people.

5. Which _____

   The Rotokas alphabet. It has only 11 letters.

6. Which _____

   English. It has about one million words.

Communication Activity

Work with a partner: Student A uses this information and Student B uses the information on page 84.

Student A
Ask questions to complete your chart.
Answer your partner's questions about some world records.

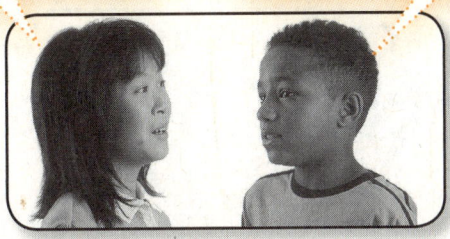

> What is the record for the hottest day?

> The record for the hottest day is 136° F (58° C) in Libya, Africa.

World Record	Who? Which?
hottest day	Libya, Africa—136° F (58° C)
number of years spent in a hospital	Martha Nelson (99 years)
number of hours flying a kite	
longest living plant	Norway spruce tree (9,550 years old)
number of first names for one person	
longest roller coaster	Steel Dragon 2000, Japan (8,133 feet)
number of hours standing on one foot	
smallest ocean	Arctic Ocean (5,440,200 square miles)
best memory	
number of uses for the peanut	George Washington Carver (300 uses)
number of teeth one animal can grow	
longest distance flown by paper airplane	Stephen Krieger, U.S.A. (207 ft., 4in./ 63.19m)
most rice eaten with chopsticks in three minutes	

Communication Activity

Work with a partner: Student B uses this information and Student A uses the information on page 83.

Student B
Answer your partner's questions about some world records.
Ask questions to complete your chart.

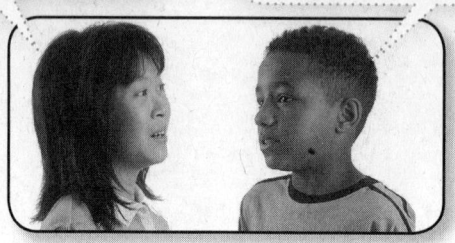

What is the record for the hottest day?

The record for the hottest day is 136° F (58° C) in Libya, Africa.

World Record	Who? Which?
hottest day	Libya, Africa—136° F (58° C)
number of years spent in a hospital	
number of hours flying a kite	Harry Osbourne (180 hours, 17 minutes)
longest living plant	
number of first names for one person	Laurence Watkins (2,310 first names)
longest roller coaster	
number of hours standing on one foot	Leslie Silva (45 hours, 25 minutes)
smallest ocean	
best memory	Bhandanta Vicitsara (16,000 pages of text)
number of uses for the peanut	
number of teeth one animal can grow	some sharks (30,000 teeth)
longest distance flown by paper airplane	
most rice eaten with chopsticks in three minutes	Tae Wah Gooding, South Korea (64 grains of rice, one at a time)

8 Mysteries Past and Present

 **1** **A. Listen to the song. Answer the questions.**

A World of Mystery

1. What mysterious things might come from space?

   _____

2. What mysterious things were carved and placed in a row?

   _____

3. What is the name of the monster that might live in Loch Ness?

   _____

4. What is the name of a mysterious circle of huge stones?

   _____

5. Where are wells that hold ancient bones?

   _____

6. What city could be under the sea?

   _____

7. What large creature have people seen walking around?

   _____

8. What city mysteriously lost its people?

   _____

B. Write. Which mystery would you like to solve? Why?

_____

_____

_____

2 Look at the symbols. What do you think they mean? Complete the sentences with words and phrases from the box. Use *could* if you are not sure of the meaning and *must* if you are sure.

    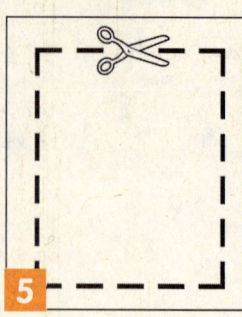

1. This _____ be a symbol for _____.
2. This symbol _____ mean _____.
3. This _____ mean _____.
4. This _____ be a symbol for _____.
5. This _____ mean _____.

close door
cut
danger
falling rocks
sadness

3 What do you think? Write sentences with *could* or *must*.

1. Why do some people abandon their cities?

_____

2. What do the drawings and paintings in ancient caves mean?

_____

3. What are the mysterious objects some people see in the sky?

_____

4. Does Nessie the Loch Ness monster exist? Why or why not?

_____

5. Why are human bones in ancient wells in the Yucatan?

_____

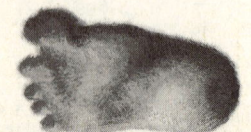 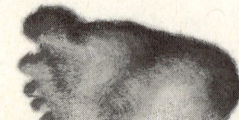 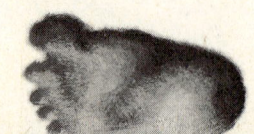

Grammar

active voice: The hikers **saw** Bigfoot.
passive voice: Bigfoot **was seen** by the hikers.

passive voice, past = *was/were* + past participle

4 **Complete the sentences with *was* or *were* and the past participle.**

1. Photographs _____ of the Loch Ness monster by a tourist.
   (taken)

2. Recently, a scientific expedition _____ to search for Nessie.
   (organized)

3. Altamira Cave _____ by a nobleman and his daughter in 1879.
   (explored)

4. Paintings in Altamira Cave _____ about 16,000 years ago.
   (made)

5. The temple of Angkor Wat _____ between 1113 and 1150 C.E.
   (constructed)

6. The temple walls _____ with beautiful stone sculptures.
   (decorated)

5 **Change each sentence into the passive voice. Use *was* or *were* + a past participle from the box.**

> built
> covered
> deserted
> forgotten
> rediscovered

1. The Incas built the great city of Machu Picchu.

   _____

2. In the 1500s, people deserted Machu Picchu.

   _____

3. Thick jungle plants covered the city.

   _____

4. People forgot the city of Machu Picchu.

   _____

5. In 1911, the explorer Hiram Bingham rediscovered Machu Picchu.

   _____

Complete the article. Use past forms in the active and passive voices.

Letterboxing

Would you like to figure out mysterious clues, search for hidden "treasure" in strange places, and collect special symbols from those places? Try letterboxing. This "treasure hunting" hobby **1** (start) _____ in 1854 by James Perrott. He **2** (hike) _____ to a wild area in southwestern England, where he **3** (put) _____ his business card in a bottle and hid it. Later, clues **4** (give) _____ to his friends to help them find the bottle. They **5** (ask) _____ to put in their own cards when they found it. That bottle **6** (become) _____ the first "letterbox" in Dartmoor National Park. People **7** (begin) _____ searching for it, and soon they started to hide other letterboxes in the park. Today, thousands of letterboxes are hidden there.

After letterboxing **8** (describe) _____ in *Smithsonian* magazine, the hobby **9** (grow) _____ popular in the United States and in other countries as well. Today, clues to letterboxes hidden around the world are published on many Internet websites. Try letterboxing!

How Letterboxing Works

A letterbox is a small, waterproof container that holds a notebook and a special stamp. Letterbox hunters use maps and clues to find the boxes. They carry their own personal stamps, ink pads, and notebooks. The finder of a letterbox puts ink on the stamp found in the letterbox and presses it into his or her notebook. Then the finder puts ink on his or her personal stamp and presses it into the notebook that is kept in the box. Finally, the finder replaces the box in its hiding place for the next person to find.

Draw your own personal stamp design!

7

Use the symbol key to write the letters of each mystery word. Then write the meaning of the word on the line.

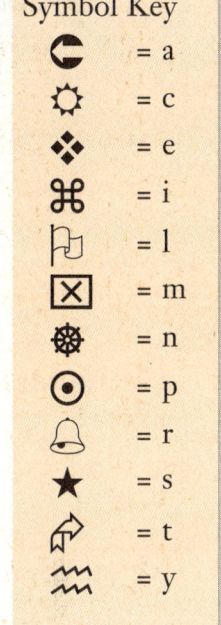

Symbol Key
- ⊂ = a
- ☼ = c
- ❖ = e
- ⌘ = i
- ⊡ = l
- ⊠ = m
- ⚙ = n
- ⊙ = p
- 🔔 = r
- ★ = s
- ⇨ = t
- 〜 = y

1. ___ ___ ___ ___ ___ ___ ___

Meaning: _____

2. ___ ___ ___ ___ ___ ___ ___

Meaning: _____

3. ___ ___ ___ ___ ___ ___

Meaning: _____

8

Find and circle words with these meanings.

a. left because of some kind of trouble
b. found again
c. very large

d. works of art made of stone, wood, or metal
e. able to do something well; expert
f. something that represents something else

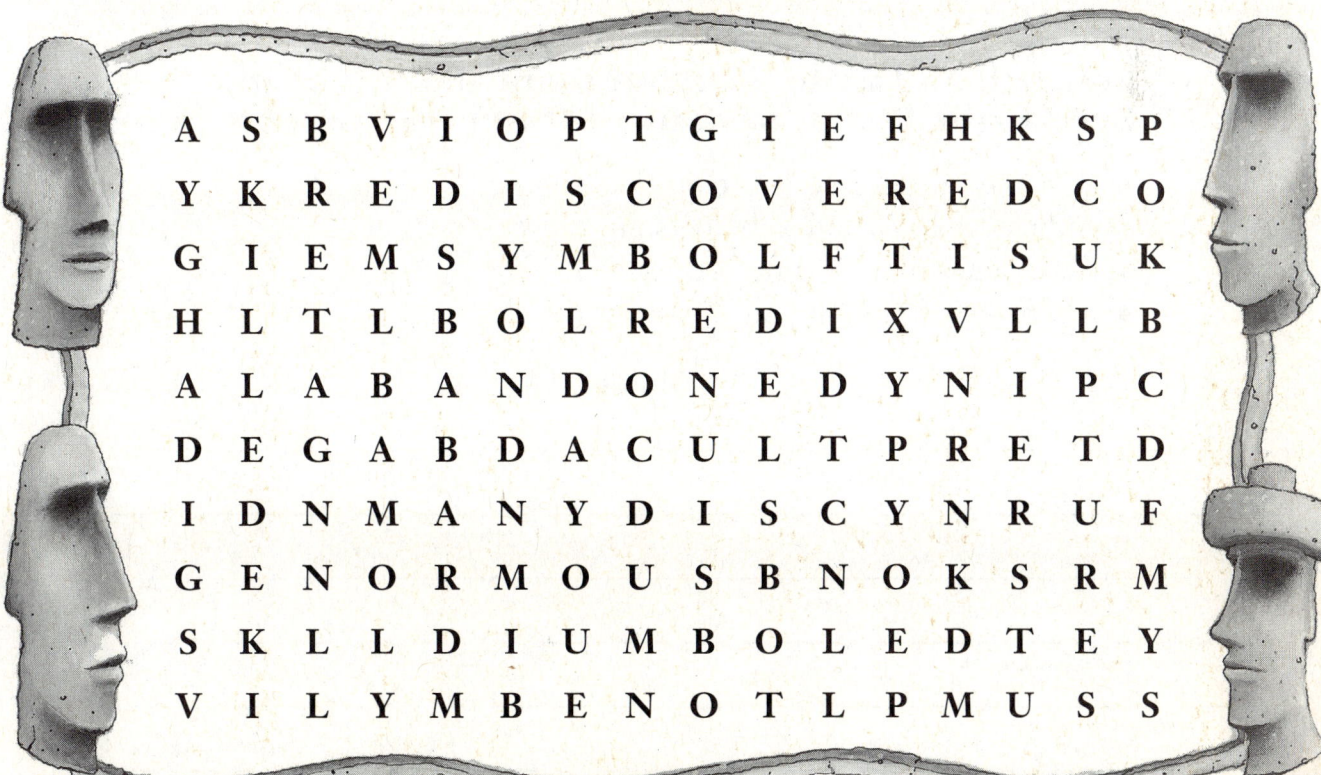

```
A S B V I O P T G I E F H K S P
Y K R E D I S C O V E R E D C O
G I E M S Y M B O L F T I S U K
H L T L B O L R E D I X V L L B
A L A B A N D O N E D Y N I P C
D E G A B D A C U L T P R E T D
I D N M A N Y D I S C Y N R U F
G E N O R M O U S B N O K S R M
S K L L D I U M B O L E D T E Y
V I L Y M B E N O T L P M U S S
```

Read *Mystery Magazine.*

 Complete the chart for the magazine story.

The Secret of Crystal Cave

The Secret of Crystal Cave		
Characters	**Setting**	**Problem**

What do you think will happen next?	**How do you think the story will end?**

10 **Research and write. Find out more about Johann Burckhardt (Petra, Jordan) or Khufu (the Great Pyramid).**

- Use the Internet, an encyclopedia, or other sources to learn about the person.
- Take notes to write a report.
- Prepare and present your report to the class.

Notes

_____

_____

_____

_____

_____

_____

_____

11 Listen. Complete the sentences.

1. The people who practice the ancient art of finding things hidden in the ground are called _____.

2. They look for substances such as _____ and _____.

3. In the old days, they usually used forked wooden sticks from _____ or _____ trees.

4. Some people didn't use sticks. Instead, they used _____ suspended over maps.

5. Today, people use L-shaped _____ or _____.

6. One theory says that changes in the earth's magnetic field might cause the _____ of the sticks.

7. Another theory says that the hidden substances might give off vibrations that cause movement in the searcher's _____, causing the stick to move.

12 Listen. Write 1–10 to show the order of the lines as you hear them.

The Riddle of the Sphinx

_____ It crouches and stares as the sun climbs high,

_____ For five thousand years the Sphinx has sat

_____ and when the sun disappears from the sky.

_____ resembling both a man and a cat.

_____ searching for answers, leaving with none.

_____ For five thousand years travelers have come

_____ Sand and silence are all the Sphinx knows.

_____ Why was it made? Who put it there?

_____ The Sphinx itself just continues to stare.

_____ With the passing of time, its mystery grows.

Writing

Paragraph of Contrast

In a paragraph of contrast, you describe how two things, people, or ideas in the same category are different. You can use adjectives to describe differences, and you can use words and expressions such as *although, but, however, in contrast, on the other hand, unlike,* and *while.*

Faces of Mystery
by Enrico Albanese

Although the ancient people of the Rapa Nui and the Olmec cultures both produced massive stone heads, there are important differences. Archaeologists think the Olmec heads are much older than those of the Rapa Nui. The earliest Olmec sculptures are believed to date from around 1200 B.C.E., **while** the Rapa Nui statues date from around 1300 C.E. The number of heads also differs. Up to now, scientists have found only twenty-two Olmec heads, **but** there are hundreds of stone heads on Rapa Nui. The stone heads differ in appearance, too. The Olmec heads are generally round, with carefully carved noses, lips, and cheeks. Expressions on the faces make them look more like different individuals, probably Olmec rulers. **On the other hand,** the hundreds of heads on Rapa Nui do not seem to represent different human beings—they resemble each other. **Unlike** the Olmec statues, they have long faces, rather than round, with long ears and noses, and triangular eyes. The mouths are often missing. Some archaeologists think they may represent an ancient god because they are so alike, though no one knows for sure. The huge stone heads of the Rapa Nui and the Olmec peoples are symbols of two ancient mysteries we may never understand completely.

Writing Assignment

Using the following steps, you will write a paragraph contrasting two things, people, or ideas that interest you.

 Brainstorm Ideas

- Pick one of these topics or a topic of your own.
  - picture writing and alphabet writing   - two animals
  - two family members   - two figures from myth or legend
  - two places   - two superheroes

- How are they different? What is interesting about them?

14 Use a Tree Diagram

A tree diagram can help you contrast two items. Each point of contrast has two "branches," one for each of the two items.

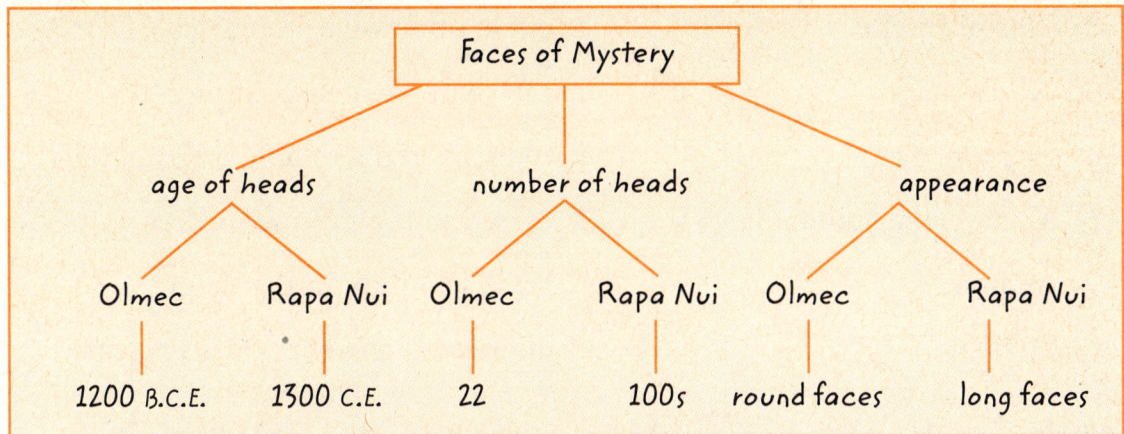

Complete a tree diagram with your ideas for your paragraph.

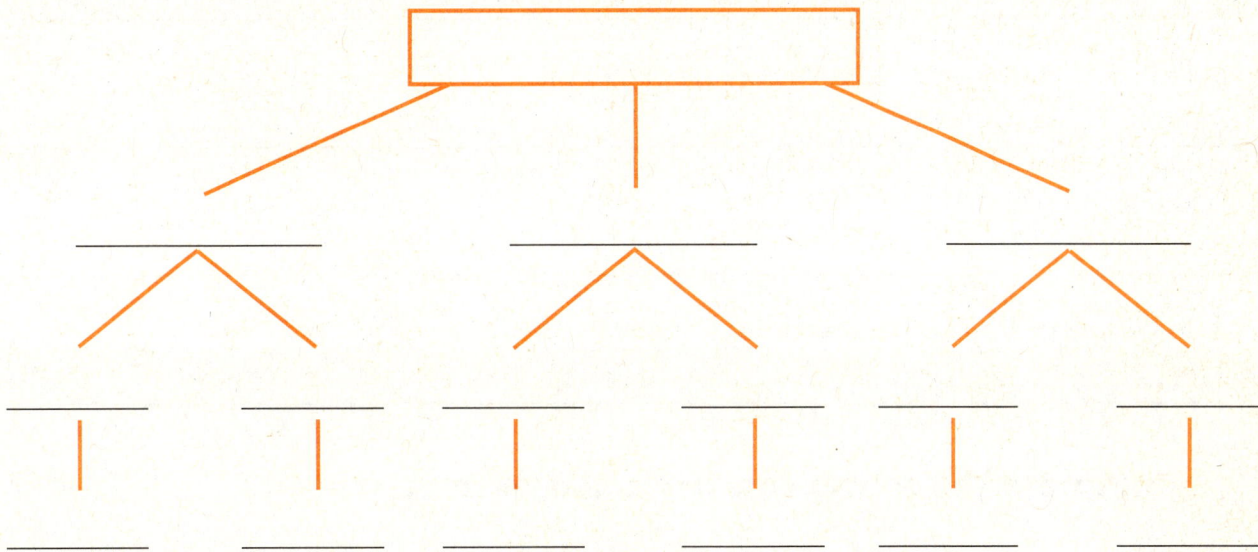

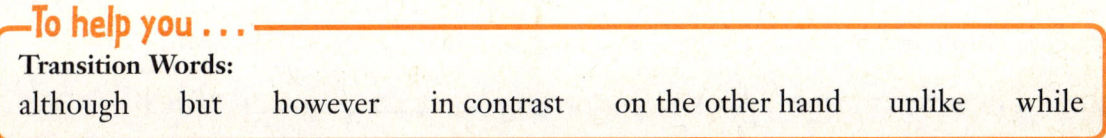

To help you . . .

Transition Words:
although   but   however   in contrast   on the other hand   unlike   while

15 Write

Use your tree diagram to help you write a paragraph of contrast. Write your paragraph on a separate piece of paper.

Review

16 **Match the names on the left with the mysteries on the right.**

_____ **1.** Stonehenge   a. abandoned city

_____ **2.** Henry Mahout   b. enormous temple

_____ **3.** Machu Picchu   c. circle of massive stones

_____ **4.** Nazca lines   d. cave with ancient paintings

_____ **5.** Angkor Wat   e. rediscovered a temple in Cambodia

_____ **6.** Marcelino de Sautuola   f. carved in the ground in Peru

_____ **7.** Altamira   g. large sculpture in the desert

_____ **8.** Sphinx   h. discovered ancient bones in a cave

17 **Write each sentence again. Use the passive voice.**

1. The Incas built the ancient city of Machu Picchu.

_____

2. Skilled artists decorated the walls of Angkor Wat.

_____

3. Ancient hunters made the paintings and handprints in Altamira Cave.

_____

4. The people of Rapa Nui carved huge statues of heads all in a row.

_____

18 **Complete the sentences. Use _could_ or _must_.**

1. Bob: I'm not sure what that is. It _____ be a UFO! What do you think?

Ben: I don't believe in UFOs. It _____ be a weather balloon.

2. Pat: I'm sure I'm right. This cave drawing _____ mean "fire."

Sue: Maybe, but it _____ mean "sun."

3. Luke: I don't know if I should go to the beach. This weather report

says it _____ rain.

Jack: You _____ have yesterday's paper. It's going to be hot all day.

Communication Activity

Work with a partner: Student A uses this information and Student B uses the information page 96.

Student A

Ask your partner questions to complete your chart.
Read the paragraph below to answer your partner's questions.

What is Timbuktu?

It is an ancient city in Mali, a country in Africa.

Timbuktu
What is Timbuktu?
Why is Timbuktu a mysterious place?
What is the city like today?
What happened in 1988?

Baalbek

Baalbek is an ancient city in Lebanon, a country in the Middle East. Baalbek was occupied by the Roman Empire and made a Roman city centuries ago. You can see that the very old Roman ruins were built on top of huge stones that were once the top part of a much older temple from an unknown culture. These enormous stones could be as much as 2,000 years older than the Roman ruins. These stones are a mystery because no one knows how it was possible to make these huge, perfect rectangles with the technology of that time. Each stone weighs about 1,500 tons and measures 68 x 14 x 14 feet. They are the largest worked stones on earth. Today, we still do not know why the stones were made or who had the skill to make them.

Communication Activity

Work with a partner: Student B uses this information and Student A uses the information page 95.

Student B
Read the paragraph below to answer your partner's questions.
Ask your partner questions to complete your chart.

What is Timbuktu?

It is an ancient city in Mali, a country in Africa.

Baalbek
What is Baalbek?
Why is Baalbek a mysterious place?
Why are the stones a mystery?
How big are the stones?

Timbuktu

Timbuktu is an ancient city in Mali, a country in Africa. In the 1200s, it was established as a place to rest and trade for people crossing the Sahara Desert on camels. The city became a legend in 1324 when the king of Mali visited Cairo, Egypt. The people there saw that the king carried a lot of gold. He told them that the gold was from Timbuktu. Over time, people began to say that the city of Timbuktu was made of gold. Many travelers tried to reach Timbuktu, but most of them disappeared and were never seen again. Hundreds of years later, some of the people who found Timbuktu were able to go home and explain that the city of gold was a myth. Today, Timbuktu is an ordinary city of fewer than 50,000 people. In 1988, it was named a World Heritage Site by the United Nations.

9 The Movies

 **A. Listen to the song. Circle T for *true* or F for *false*.**

How About a Movie?

1. Jeff said *The Mummy* wasn't scary enough.   T   F
2. Jane said *Love Lost* was a bore.   T   F
3. Tom said *Robot Teacher* was cool.   T   F
4. He thought *The Brothers from Mars* wasn't so great.   T   F
5. Jim said *Spy Teens 1* was fantastic.   T   F

B. Write another verse. Here are some movie titles and words you can use.

Titles	Words	
Grandparents from Mars	a long wait	ghastly
New Love	before	picks
Return of the Monster	eight	six
Robot Student	four	three

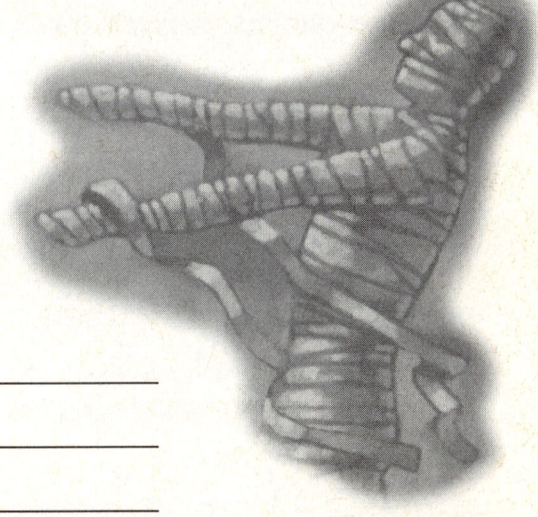

_____

_____

_____

_____

_____

_____

_____

2 A. Is it a positive or a negative word? Write each word in the correct column of the chart.

☺ Positive Words	☹ Negative Words
1. cool	6.
2.	7.
3.	8.
4.	9.
5.	10.

awful   confusing
cool   exciting
fantastic great
horrible   silly
terrible   wonderful

B. Read the comments about the movies. Write one positive and one negative word.

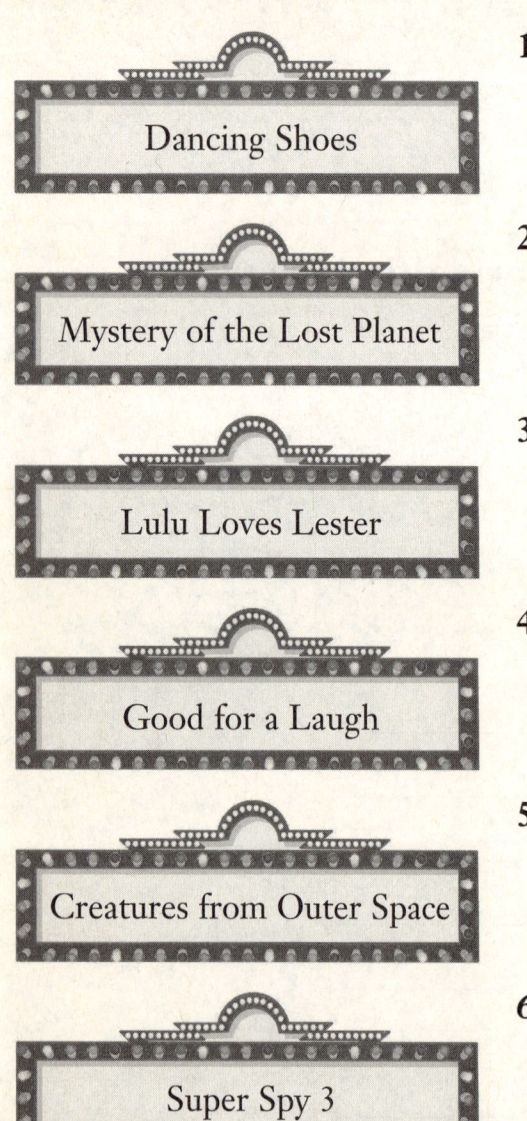

Dancing Shoes

Mystery of the Lost Planet

Lulu Loves Lester

Good for a Laugh

Creatures from Outer Space

Super Spy 3

1. How about seeing *Dancing Shoes*?

   Pat: No, that musical is too _____.

   Bill: Yes, it's so _____!

2. How about *Mystery of the Lost Planet*?

   Ken: No, that movie is too _____.

   Sue: Yes, it is so _____.

3. Why don't we see *Lulu Loves Lester*?

   Ana: No, I heard the acting is _____.

   Bob: Yes, that sounds _____!

4. How about *Good for a Laugh*?

   Lee: No, I heard the jokes are _____.

   Tim: Yes, I heard it's _____!

5. What about *Creatures from Outer Space*?

   Dan: No, the creatures look _____.

   Jill: Yes, it sounds _____.

6. Why don't we see *Super Spy 3*?

   Tom: No, Sara said the acting was _____.

   Lucy: Yes, Jim said it was _____.

Original statement	Reported speech
Laura: "This action film **is** exciting."	Laura said the action film **was** exciting.
Carl: "I **love** this scary part."	Carl said he **loved** the scary part.
Gina: "I **don't like** the special effects."	Gina said she **didn't like** the special effects.

③ Write sentences in reported speech.

1. Ingrid: "This love story is silly."

   _____

2. Bill: "I love the music."

   _____

3. Jane: "The acting isn't great."

   _____

4. Cara: "I don't like the ending."

   _____

Grammar

Original statement	Reported speech
Ben: "I **have** never **seen** such a funny movie."	Ben said he **had** never **seen** such a funny movie.
Sara: "I **haven't seen** it yet."	Sara said she **hadn't seen** it yet.
Matt: "I **have** never **laughed** so much."	Matt said he **had** never **laughed** so much.

④ Write sentences in reported speech.

1. Sue: "I have never seen such an exciting movie."

   _____

2. Dale: "I have seen that one three times."

   _____

3. Bob: "I haven't been to any of these movies."

   _____

4. Kate: "I have bought a ticket for the science fiction movie."

   _____

5. Dee: "I have waited in this line for two hours."

   _____

5 **Read the reported speech. Write the original statement. Use quotation marks.**

Pablo said he loved mysteries.	Dan said he liked the acting.
Luz said she wanted to see a comedy.	Sara said she didn't have a ticket for the movie.

 "I love mysteries."

Pablo   Luz   Dan   Sara

Grammar

| **Original speech** | **Reported statement** |
| Joe: "I **haven't been** to the movies in a month." | Joe said he **hadn't been** to the movies in a month. |

6 **Write the missing sentences in each column.**

Original Statement	Reported Speech
1. Ben: "I have read only good reviews of this movie."	1. _____ _____
2. Mario: _____ _____	2. Mario said he hadn't seen any musicals so far.
3. Kala: "I have seen two movies with special effects."	3. _____ _____
4. Will: _____ _____	4. Will said he hadn't bought the movie tickets.

7 A. Unscramble and write the words.

1. D O E C M Y ⭘ _ _ ⭘ _ _
2. Y S T R M E Y _ _ ⭘ _ _ _ _
3. A U M C S I L _ _ _ _ ⭘⭘ _
4. I C A T N O   L M I F _ _ _ ⭘ _ _ ⭘⭘ _ _
5. V E L O   O T S R Y _ _ _ ⭘ _ ⭘ _ _
6. C E S N I C E   N I C T I O F _ _ _ _ ⭘ _ _ ⭘ _ _ _ _

B. Write the circled letters below.

_ _ _ _ _ _ _ _ _ _ _ _ _ P

C. Now unscramble the circled letters. Use the letters to make two words that will complete the sentence.

"Science fiction movies have great __ P _ _ _ _ _   _ _ _ _ _ _ _ ."

8 Write about a movie you saw. Use at least two words from the box.

awful	bold	boring	cool	confusing
dull	exciting	fantastic	funny	great
horrible	scary	silly	terrible	

Movie: _____

Kind of Movie: _____

Actors: _____

Opinion: _____

_____

_____

_____

_____

_____

Read *Movie Magazine*.

9 **Circle T for *true* or F for *false*. Rewrite the false statements correctly on the lines below.**

Inside C3PO & R2D2

1. Many people recognize the faces of the two British actors from their appearances as C3PO and R2D2 in *Star Wars*.   T   F

2. R2D2 is a robot that looks human.   T   F

3. Filmmakers said they wanted people to know that C3PO was an actor in a suit.   T   F

4. The actor who plays R2D2 must use remote controls to move around.   T   F

_____

_____

_____

_____

10 **List three pieces of advice that *MM* gives to Sheila.**

Our Readers' Mail

1. _____

2. _____

3. _____

11 **Research and write. Find out about your favorite child actor. Do research in the library and on the Internet to find out how he or she became an actor. Write a paragraph using what you found out.**

_____
(title)

_____

_____

_____

_____

12 **Listen. Circle T for *true* or F for *false*.**

1. *Movie Moments* is a popular TV show.   T   F

2. Tonight's guest is a controversial director.   T   F

3. Michael Mordant makes documentaries.   T   F

4. His latest film is about death in hospitals.   T   F

5. Mordant wanted to upset people with his film.   T   F

6. Mordant believes children's futures are at risk.   T   F

13   **A. Listen. Write the word or words that answer the questions.**

Pretty Good, Don't You Think?

1. How was the lighting? _____

2. How was the acting? _____

3. How was the story? _____

4. How was the music? _____

5. How did the "teenager" actor look?

   _____

6. How was the "action hero"? _____,

   not _____

7. How was the popcorn? _____

8. How was the soda? _____

9. How was the seat? _____, _____,

   _____, and _____

B. Write some new lines about another movie. Write the title.

Title: _____

You've got to be kidding! What did I hear?

We clearly just saw the _____ film of the year!

The _____ was _____ and the _____ was _____.

The story was _____ and the _____ was _____.

Writing

Letter to the Editor

When you read something you strongly agree or disagree with in a magazine or newspaper, you can write a letter to the editor to express your opinion. In your letter, mention the statement or article you are reacting to, give your own opinion, and include facts, reasons, or examples that support your opinion. Don't forget to identify who you are.

> To the Editor:
>
> In his April third column, movie reviewer Bud Marks said that children these days go to the movies for the special effects and nothing else. As a sixth-grader who goes to the movies once a week, I have to disagree. I believe that Mr. Marks underestimates us. We young people are smarter than Mr. Marks thinks!
>
> Special effects can be very exciting, but we know that a movie with nothing else is not a very good movie. For example, we appreciate an interesting story line and good acting. We enjoy examples of humor, drama, and suspense. We like thinking about important life issues such as good versus evil, honor, loyalty, and friendship.
>
> In my film club at school, we choose good movies to see. Only three of the ten movies we saw this year were filled with spectacular special effects, but even those three had good stories to tell. And we often chose movies that were based on books so that we could compare the movie and book versions. We enjoyed ourselves and we learned a lot.
>
> In my opinion, Mr. Marks needs to talk to more children about movies before he makes another statement that underestimates us as moviegoers.
>
> Sincerely,
> Mike Henderson

Writing Assignment

Using the following steps, you will write a letter to the editor to express your opinion.

 Brainstorm Ideas

- Choose a statement to react to or find one in a newspaper or magazine.
  A. "It is important to protect children from scary and violent television shows. TV programs need the same kind of rating systems that our movies have." *Sarah Byrne, newspaper columnist*
  B. "The video games, TV shows, and movies our children like cause them to have short attention spans, read less, and do less well in school." *John Rosario, school principal, magazine interview*

Use a Letter Template

A template can help you organize your ideas.

To the Editor:

Paragraph One

Sentence 1: date of statement, author of statement, reported statement
Sentence 2: who you are and how you relate to the topic, statement of
             agreement or disagreement
Sentence 3: your main point

Paragraph Two

Sentence 1: first reason you agree or disagree with the statement
Sentence 2: example or explanation
Sentence 3: additional example or explanation
Sentence 4: additional example or explanation

Paragraph Three

Sentence 1: second reason you agree or disagree with the statement
Sentence 2: example or explanation
Sentence 3: additional example or explanation
Sentence 4: additional example or explanation

Paragraph Four

Sentence: restatement of your main point

Sincerely,
(*your name*)

To help you . . .

Expressions:
I agree   I believe   I disagree   I think   in my opinion

 **Write**

Use your template to help you write a final draft of your letter to the editor. Use a
separate piece of paper.

Review

17 **Read what five friends said about the movie *Mars Adventure*. Then write sentences. Use reported speech.**

Friends	Their Opinions
1. Millie	"I don't like it at all."
2. Tim	"It's too silly."
3. Janie	"The acting is really bad."
4. Dale	"The story isn't exiting."
5. Carla	"It's the worst movie I've ever seen."

1. _____

2. _____

3. _____

4. _____

5. _____

18 **Imagine you've just seen the movie *Sea Monsters*. Was it good or bad? Write a good review or a bad review. Use categories and opinion words from the boxes.**

Categories	
acting	ending
lighting	music
special effects	story

Opinion Words	
best	boring
confusing	cool
fantastic	great
scary	silly
terrible	worst

Sea Monsters: **The** _____ **Movie of the Year!**

_____

_____

_____

_____

_____

_____

Communication Activity

Work with a partner: Student A uses this page and Student B uses page 108.

Student A

A. Ask your partner for the titles of two movies he or she has seen. List them.

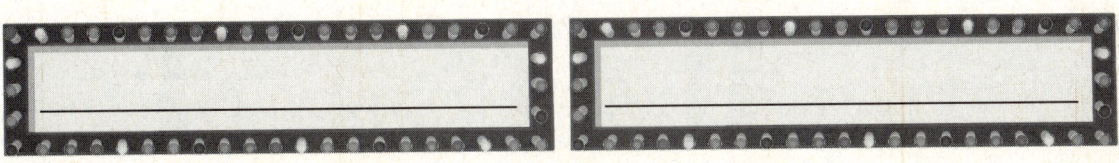

B. Ask your partner about one of the movies. List what he or she liked and didn't like.

Movie: _____

Likes	Dislikes

C. Write a brief summary of your partner's opinions. Use reported speech.

_____

_____

_____

_____

_____

_____

Communication Activity

Work with a partner: Student B uses this page and Student A uses page 107.

Student B

A. Ask your partner for the titles of two movies he or she has seen. List them.

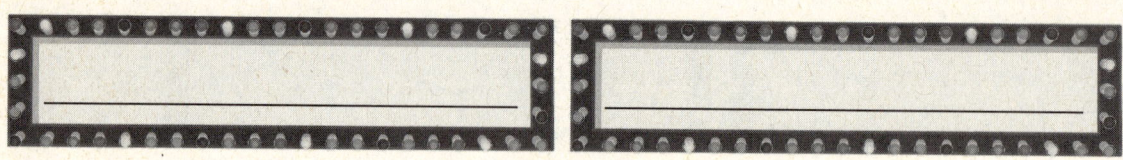

B. Ask your partner about one of the movies. List what he or she liked and didn't like.

Movie: _____

Likes	Dislikes

C. Write a brief summary of your partner's opinions. Use reported speech.

_____

_____

_____

_____

_____

Grammar Handbook

1 **The Simple Past:** Write the simple past forms of *jump* and *make*.

Regular verb: _____   Irregular verb: _____

I _____   we _____   I _____   we _____

you _____   you _____   you _____   you _____

he/she/it _____   they _____   he/she/it _____   they _____

2 **Irregular Verbs in the Simple Past:** Write the simple past forms.

1. become   _____   7. hear   _____

2. begin   _____   8. keep   _____

3. build   _____   9. leave   _____

4. come   _____   10. lose   _____

5. fly   _____   11. see   _____

6. get   _____   12. take   _____

3 **The Simple Past:** Change the affirmative verb forms to the negative.

1. Carlos Diaz *was born* in Quito, Ecuador.   _____

2. Isilay Davaz *began* flying at age three.   _____

3. J. Hurlinger *walked* 800 miles on his hands.   _____

4. Josh Lee *rode* a mule across the Grand Canyon.   _____

4 **Questions:** Write questions for the answers.

1. _____

   Sarah Chang won the Nan Pa Award *in 1991*.

2. _____

   Jackie Chan studied *singing, acting, and martial arts*.

3. _____

   J.K. Rowling wrote the first Harry Potter book *in a Scottish café*.

4. _____

   Michel Lotito ate the wood and metal coffin *piece by piece*.

1 **The Simple Past and The Present Perfect:** Check the boxes for the meaning.

	completed action	continuing action
1. Luke played the drums in the school band.	☐	☐
2. Yoko has lived in Chicago since 2005.	☐	☐
3. We have had our dog Spot for three years now.	☐	☐
4. I studied for the science test for two hours.	☐	☐

2 **Past Participles:** Write the correct forms.

1. attend _____
2. earn _____
3. get _____
4. go _____
5. grow _____
6. lose _____

7. love _____
8. spend _____
9. visit _____
10. wear _____
11. win _____
12. write _____

3 **The Simple Past and The Present Perfect:** Complete the sentences with the correct form.

1. (do) What _____ you _____ last weekend?
2. (know) Greg _____ my family for years.
3. (meet) My mom _____ my dad in 1997.
4. (play) Sam and Mark _____ soccer for 3 years, and they love it.
5. (be) Mary _____ here since 2:00.

4 **For and since:** Write the correct word.

1. _____ ten minutes
2. _____ 2007
3. _____ two days

4. _____ first grade
5. _____ I was little
6. _____ a month

Grammar Handbook

1 **Gerunds:** Complete the sentences.

1. (paint) I enjoy _____. It's relaxing.

2. (get) Billy is worried about _____ good grades.

3. (swim) _____ is great exercise for all your muscles.

4. (take) Kim is interested in _____ piano lessons.

5. (play) _____ chess develops strategic thinking.

6. (eat) Sandra gave up _____ candy last week.

2 **Present True Conditionals:** Circle the condition and underline the result clause.

1. I'll buy a new guitar if I get money for my birthday.

2. If Dan continues to work hard, he'll do very well on the final exam.

3 **Present True Conditionals:** Complete the sentences.

1. If I _____ a lot, I _____ a good singer one day.
   (practice)   (be)

2. If we _____, we _____ the next bus.
   (hurry)   (catch)

3. David _____ Lucy with math if she _____ it.
   (help)   (need)

4. We _____ to the game if we _____ time.
   (go)   (have)

5. _____ you _____ in the school play if they _____ you?
              (act)   (ask)

4 **Present True Conditionals:** Write complete sentences with *if*.

1. Fact: You want to call me tonight.
   Fact: I am home at 7:00.

   _____

2. Fact: We can buy the food.
   Fact: Ramona cooks.

   _____

1 **Certainty:** Write predictions with *will, won't, may, could,* and *might*.

1. (100% sure) schools/disappear/future

   _____

2. (50% sure) personal robots/replace/people

   _____

3. (50% sure) people/live/moon

   _____

4. (100% sure) people/take/vacations/in space

   _____

5. (50% sure) clothes/have/built-in computers

   _____

6. (50% sure) people/read/each other's minds

   _____

2 **Causative *have*:** Write complete sentences with *will* and *have*.

1. I don't know how to pull my tooth. (dentist)

   _____

2. Kendra doesn't know how to cook her food. (chef)

   _____

3. They don't know how to fix the electricity. (electrician)

   _____

4. James doesn't want to cut his own hair. (barber)

   _____

5. I want another cup of tea. (waiter)

   _____

6. In the future, my grandchildren won't do homework. (robot)

   _____

Grammar Handbook

1   **Superlatives:** Complete the sentences with a superlative and a noun.

1. (windy) The _____ is Neptune.

2. (smart) The _____ is Ken.

3. (big) The _____ is the blue whale.

2   *The most* **+ Noun:** Complete the sentences with *the most* and a noun.

1. The planet with _____ is Jupiter.

2. The planet with _____ is Saturn.

3   **Present Untrue Conditionals:** Complete the sentences with *would* and the verbs.

1. We don't travel in time.

   If we _____ (travel) in time, we _____ (visit) both the past and the future.

2. Roberto doesn't have a telescope.

   If he _____ (have) a telescope, he _____ (see) the stars and planets much more clearly.

3. My brothers aren't interested in space.

   If they _____ (be) interested in space, they _____ (go) to the Space Museum with me.

4. I am not inside a black hole.

   What _____ (happen) if you _____ (fall) into a black hole?

4   **Present Untrue Conditionals:** Use *if* and *would*.

1. I don't have a lot of money.

   _____

2. My family doesn't have time to travel.

   _____

Grammar Handbook

1 **The Present Perfect:** Complete the present perfect forms.

Regular: *climb*

I _____ we _____

you _____ you _____

he/she/it _____ they _____

Irregular: *ride*

I _____ we _____

you _____ you _____

he/she/it _____ they _____

2 **The Present Perfect:** Complete the sentences.

1. Jane _____ (see) a volcano erupt!

2. We _____ (go) to Peru twice.

3. I _____ (swim) in an underwater cave.

4. _____ you ever _____ (fly) in a helicopter?

3 **The Present Perfect with** *already, never,* **and** *yet*: Complete the sentences with *already, never,* or *yet* and other words.

1. Have you ever gone hiking in a rain forest?

No, _____, and I don't want to.

2. Have you ever traveled to another country?

Yes, _____, and it was great.

3. Have you ever won a race?

No, _____, but I will one day!

4 *Would* + *ever* + **Verb:** Write questions and complete answers.

1. (go snowboarding) _____

_____

2. (eat a live insect) _____

_____

3. (hold a snake) _____

_____

1 **Approximation:** Which quantities are exact? Which are approximate? Check the boxes.

	exact	approximate
1. The dinosaurs died out around 65 million years ago.	☐	☐
2. Sharks can grow more than 30,000 teeth in their lifetimes.	☐	☐
3. The last Pyrenean ibex died in Spain in January of 2000.	☐	☐
4. The seahorse moves .001 miles (.002 km.) per hour.	☐	☐

2 *More/fewer* + **Noun:** Complete the sentences.

1. The Hawaiian alphabet has 14 letters. The English alphabet has 26 letters.

   The Hawaiian alphabet _____

2. Camels have six eyelids. Humans have two eyelids.

   Camels _____

3. Gary Duschl collected over 1,000,000 gum wrappers. Peggy Moller collected

   613,594. Gary Duschl _____

4. Vatican City has around 890 people. Peru has around 29,200,000 people.

   Vatican City _____

3 The *most/fewest* + **Noun:** Complete the sentences.

1. Tokyo has about 28,000,000 people, Mexico City 18,000,000, and New York 16,000,000.

   Tokyo _____

2. Humans have two legs, tigers have four, and spiders have eight.

   Humans _____

3. A soccer team has eleven members, a baseball team has nine, and a volleyball team has six.

   A volleyball team _____

4. Spinner dolphins have 252 teeth, giant armadillos have 100, and humans have 32.

   Spinner dolphins _____

1 **Certainty with** *must*: Write sentences with *must, may, could,* and *might.*

1. (100% sure) phone call / for me

_____

2. (50% sure) no light in the window / not at home

_____

3. (100% sure) Alan / not in school / sick

_____

4. (50% sure) he / bag of money / thief

_____

2 **Past Participles:** Write the forms.

1. build _____   5. leave _____

2. desert _____   6. lose _____

3. find _____   7. make _____

4. forget _____   8. tell _____

3 **The Passive Voice in the Past:** Complete the sentences.

1. Machu Picchu _____ (rediscover) in 1911.

2. The Altamira cave paintings _____ (make) over 16,000 years ago.

3. The temple of Angkor Wat _____ (abandon) around 1431 C.E.

4. The Nazca lines in Peru _____ (carve) centuries ago.

4 **The Passive Voice in the Past:** Change the sentences to the passive voice.

1. The United Nations named the city of Timbuktu a World Heritage Site in 1988.

_____

2. People discovered enormous stone rectangles in the ancient city of Baalbek.

_____

1 **Invitations:** Write complete sentences.

1. watch / *Your Idol* / on TV (why)

_____

2. go / soccer game / at 6:00 (how)

_____

3. go shopping / new mall (let)

_____

4. have / dinner / vegetarian restaurant (how)

_____

5. play / chess / after school (would)

_____

2 **Reported Speech:** Change the quoted speech to reported speech.

1. Lucy: "I really like horror movies."

_____

2. Bart: "I hate green vegetables."

_____

3. Pilar and Ana: "We enjoyed the salsa concert."

_____

4. Steve: "My team has won the first soccer game of the year."

_____

5. Li and Jack: "We have finished our science project."

_____

3 **Reported Speech:** Report one thing your teacher says to you.

_____

Prewriting

1 Try free writing. Write about **sports** without stopping for three to five minutes. Even if you can't think of anything to say, you have to keep on writing. When you come to the end of a sentence and you don't have another sentence ready in your mind, repeat the last sentence again. If you don't know a word you need in English, just write that word in your native language and then continue in English. *Don't stop.*

2 Look over your free writing. Is there the beginning of an idea that you could develop further into a good focused topic and main idea? How did you like free writing?

Writing the First Draft

1 Choose one of the topics.

A Terrible Day   Exercise   Global Warming   My Family   The Internet   Volcanoes

2 For the topic you chose, decide *why* you are writing, *who* you are writing for, and *what type* of writing you will do. Write in the chart.

Purpose	
Audience	
Form	

3 Focus your topic and narrow it down to a manageable size for writing. Then decide on one main idea about the focused topic to write about.

4 Create a good beginning, middle, and end for your focused topic and main idea. Write your first draft here.

Revising

1 Read aloud to yourself the first draft you wrote on page 119. Then share it with a writing partner. Listen to your partner's comments and suggestions. Decide if you need to add details, to add transition words, to change the order of any sentences, to take out unrelated or repetitive sentences, or to rewrite sentences that aren't clear or interesting.

2 Write a second draft with the changes you think it needs.

_____

_____

_____

_____

_____

_____

_____

_____

_____

_____

_____

_____

_____

_____

_____

3 Share your second draft with your writing partner. Compare each other's first and second drafts. Are the changes real improvements? Are the ideas and organization better in your second drafts?

Editing and Proofreading

1 Work with a writing partner. Give the second draft of your writing from page 120 to your partner. Take your partner's second draft to work with.

2 Edit and proofread your partner's writing. Be sure to check style by looking for sentence variety, parallelism, and word choice. Check grammar, punctuation, capitalization, and spelling. Make any necessary changes.

3 When you are finished, exchange drafts again. Look at your partner's changes and comments about your work. Do you agree with all of them? Make a clean copy of your corrected draft here, or glue your draft with corrections here.

Publishing

1 With your classmates, form groups according to the topic you chose to write about.

A Terrible Day   Exercise   Global Warming   My Family   The Internet   Volcanoes

2 Each group will make a class book of all the writing on the same topic. There will be six class books, one for each of the six topics.

3 In your group, decide whose writing will go first, second, third, and so on. Make a Table of Contents page for your class book. It should have a numbered list of the titles of the writing pieces, followed by the names of the authors, and page numbers.

Table of Contents

1. Global Warming Is Serious   page 3
   by Sara Kennedy

2. Help Our Warming World   page 4
   by Manolo Hurtado

3. The Myth of Global Warming   page 5
   by Lee-Young Park

4 Make and decorate a cover for your class book. Make the title of the book the same as or similar to the topic your group wrote about. Collect clean final copies of each piece.

5 Punch holes in all the pages and the cover. Thread string or metal rings through all the holes to hold the front cover, back cover, and interior pages together.

6 When your book is ready, use a tape recorder to make an audio book. Read your writing in your best, expressive voice for your recording. When everyone has recorded the reading of their work, label the tape with the title of the book.

7 Put your tape recording and class book in a large, transparent plastic bag. Keep all the class books and recordings on a classroom shelf for students to enjoy.

8 You're published!